FITTER SECOND YEAR MCQ

OBJECTIVE QUESTION ANSWERS

MANOJ DOLE

Digitization is the need of the time. In the future, training in industrial training institutes will need to be conducted using online internet to make training more convenient and easy. E-books containing a set of MCQ questions will be made available to the trainees as they need to be more accustomed to the multiple choice questions MCQ to prepare for the online exams taking place in their industrial training institutes.

With all these factors in mind, Mr. Manoj Madhukar Dole Instructor, Industrial Training Institute, Satara, has written books according to the new annual system and NSQF-5 syllabus. And they've created theoretical mobile apps and blogs to make training easier, and made all these educational materials available for download on the world famous websites Google Play Store, Amazon and Apple Book Store.

The books were published by Hon'ble Joint Director Shri Rajendra Ghume Saheb Regional Office of Vocational Education and Training, Pune on 9/1/2019, at this time Shri Prakash Saigavkar Saheb Principal Government Industrial Training Institute Aundh Pune, Shri Tukaram Misal Saheb Principal Govt. Q. Sanstha Satara, Shri Sachin Dhumal Saheb District Vocational Education and Training Officer Satara, Shri Yatin Pargaonkar Saheb Principal Govt. Q. Sanstha Kolhapur, Shri Vikas Teke Saheb Inspector Vocational Education and Training Regional Office Pune, Palekar Foods Products Pvt. Ltd. Entrepreneurial Chairman of Satara Mr. Nilkanthrao Palekar Saheb, Chairman of Hira Foods Mr. Ibrahim Baba Tamboli Saheb, Mrs. Shalmali Pawar Headmaster Government Technical School Center Satara and other dignitaries were present on the occasion.

Contents

Prologue

Fitter Second Year MCQ is a simple e-Book for ITI Engineering Course Fitter, Second Year, Sem- 3 & 4, Revised NSQ F-5 Syllabus in 2022, It contains objective questions with underlined & bold correct answers MCQ covering all topics including all about the latest & Important about Power tool operation, different complex assembling and fitting, fastening, lapping, making gauges, pipe works and pipe joints, Dismantling, overhauling & assembling valves, Making & using drill jigs, making of critical components, repair & maintenance of power transmission system, making of template &complex gauges, identify different Pneumatic & hydraulic components and circuit construction, repair & maintenance of machinery like lathe, drill, grinding, bench drilling and lots more.

We add new question answers with each new version. Please email us in case of any errors/omissions. This is arguably the largest and best e-Book for All engineering multiple choice questions and answers.

As a student you can use it for your exam prep. This e-Book is also useful for professors to refresh material.

Foreword

Vocational education and training is imparted through the Department of Vocational Education and Training through the Department of Business Education and Business Practical to supply multi-skilled artisans in line with the rapidly growing demand in the industrial sector in the 21st century. All the occupations within the institutions are important, as the trainees from these occupations develop multi-skills as per the demands of the industry.

with the noble intention of making available MCQ e-books suitable for all businesses, considering that all the examinations in all the industries in the industrial sector are conducted online and include MCQ method questions. Mr. Manoj Madhukar Dole has written a very good e-book on MCQ method as per the new annual syllabus. This e-book will definitely be a guide for all the trainees, trainee candidates, training instructors and others concerned.

The author of the book is Mr. Manoj Madhukar Dole, Instructor Gov. ITI Satara has 17 years of training experience. Written as a new annual pattern, this e-book incorporates modern digital QR Code technology to understand the layout, simple language, and simple syntax, diagrams and videos for each subject. So I am sure that this e-book will definitely be useful for in-depth study and exam practice. The work they have done is certainly commendable.

Mr. Tukaram Misal
Principal Government Industrial Training Institute Satara.

Preface

DGET New Delhi and CSTARI Kolkata have been implementing an annual pattern for all businesses in ITI since the August 2018 session. The examination system will also be changed and it will be online from this year and since all the questions are of Objective Type (MCQ), the trainees are in dire need of in-depth study. It is with this in mind that we are delighted to present the books based on the old NIMI pattern and a complete overview of the new annual pattern, and we hope that these books will be a guide for all business directors and trainees. Is.

For writing these books, Johar Awate Saheb, Principal of ITI Akluj. Former Principal of ITI Satara Saigavkar Saheb, Assistant Director Shri Chandrakant Dhekne Saheb Regional Office of Vocational Education and Training, Pune, District Vocational Education and Training Officer Sachin Dhumal Saheb and Headmaster Government Technical School Kendra Shalmali Pawar Madam and son Adhiraj Dole, mother Kusum Dole, I am very grateful to my father Madhukar Dole and wife Ashwini Dole for their special guidance and cooperation from time to time.

Also, in a very short period of time, the book was reviewed by Shri Rajendra Ghume Saheb, Joint Director, Vocational Education and Training Regional Office, Pune, for his invaluable time in publishing the book. I am sincerely grateful for their feedback.

I am grateful to the Instructor of ITI Satara for there continuous support from the very beginning of writing the book.

From this book, I consider myself blessed to have shared my thoughts on e-learning with you. I will not claim that this book is perfect, because considering the perfection, this book is an attempt and is in its infancy. They will be valuable for improvement if they are tested and suggested.

Manoj Dole
Dated 9/1/2019

Acknowledgements

The industrial training and theoretical examination system of our industrial training institutes and these changes have been accepted by the craft instructors and the trainees. Theoretical examinations conducted in your industrial training institutes are also conducted online. Since these examinations are of multiple choice MCQ method, the trainees will need to get more practice of such questions.

With all these considerations in mind, Mr. Manoj Madhukar, Director, Dole Crafts, Katari Industrial Training Institute, Satara, has done a thorough study and with his diligent work and added his keen intellect, according to the new annual system and NSQF-5 syllabus, e-book of Katari and other machine trades. -Book) and they have created mobile apps and blogs on theoretical topics to make training easier and have made all these educational materials available for download on the world famous websites Google Play Store, Amazon and Apple Book Store. Training has been made easier by creating a print version and using advanced techniques like QR Code.

All these educational materials will definitely be a guide for all the trainees for in-depth study and for the craft instructors and other concerned who are imparting vocational training.

CHAPTER ONE

Fitter Second Year MCQ Drawing

Online Test Exam
ITI Books
CNC Course
AutoCAD CAM
JOB & Apprentice
Online Theory
Computer Course
Trading Course
Web Designing
MSCIT Course
Shopping Business
Internet Business
Remotasks Course
Online Services
Top Sportsmans
Indian Army
Freedom Fighters
Top Scientists
Social Reformers
Motivational Speaker
Top Richest People
Join WhatsApp Group
Join Facebook Group
Like Facebook Page
PAN / Adhar / Licence Passport

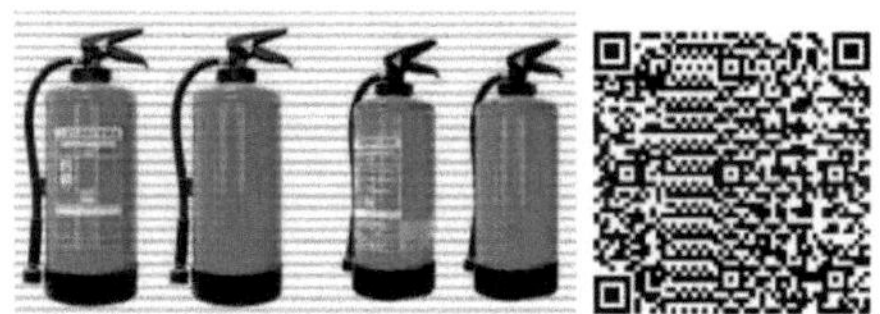

Fire extinguisher

Calliper

Hacksaw frame

Universal surface guage

Hammer

Centre punch

Bench vice

Files

Scraper

Surface Plate

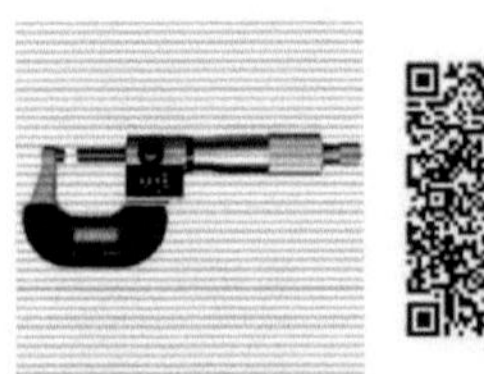

Outside Micrometer

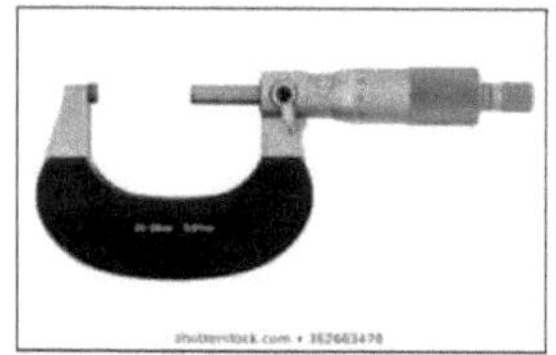

Micrometer

Depth micrometer

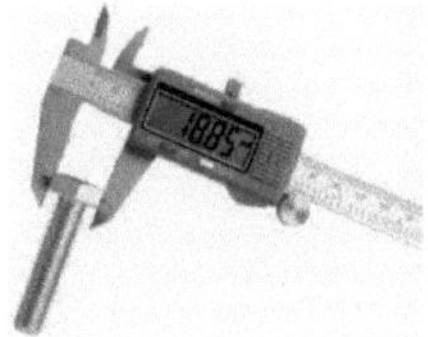

Vernier Calliper

Vernier bevel protractor

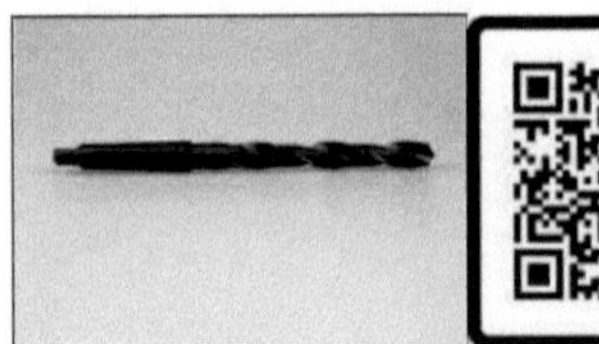

Drilling

Reamer

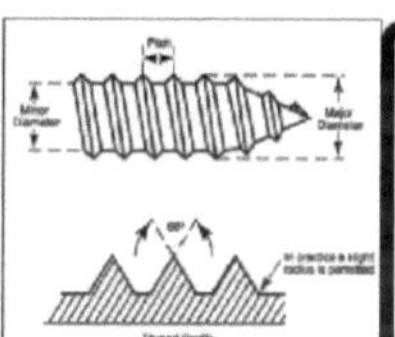

Thread

Tap Die

Grinding Wheel

Slip gauge

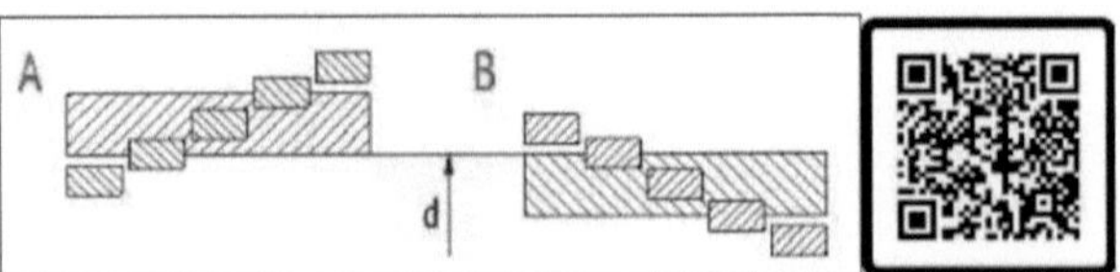

Limit fit tolerance

Lathe Machine

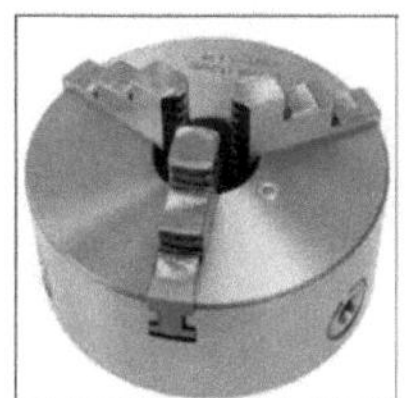

Lathe chuck

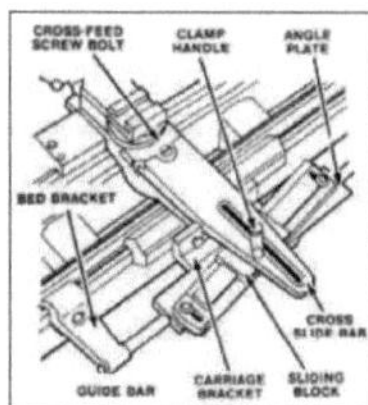

Taper turning attachment

taper ring gauge

screw pitch gauge

Gear

screw pitch gauge

Tap Die

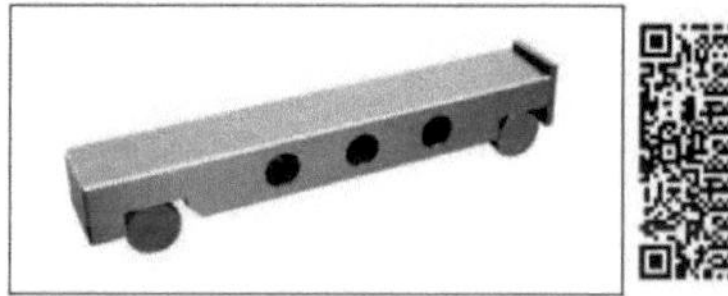

Sine bar

Slip gauge

Dial test indicator

Telescopic gauge

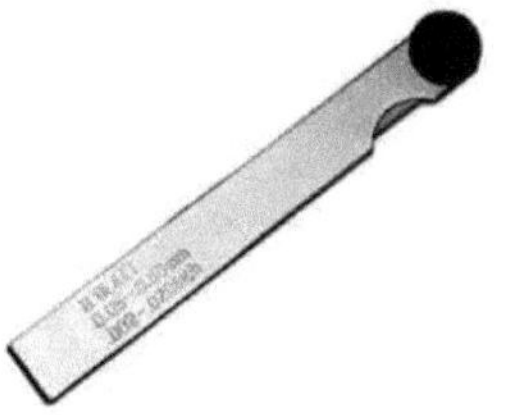

Feeler gauge

Centre gauge

Jig

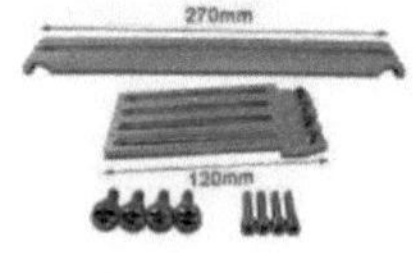

Fixture

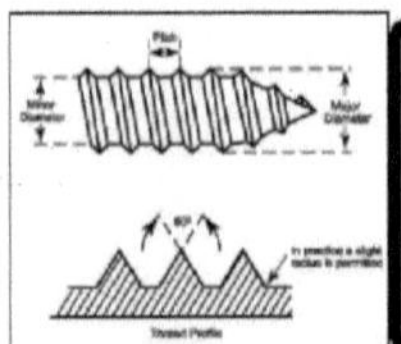

Thread

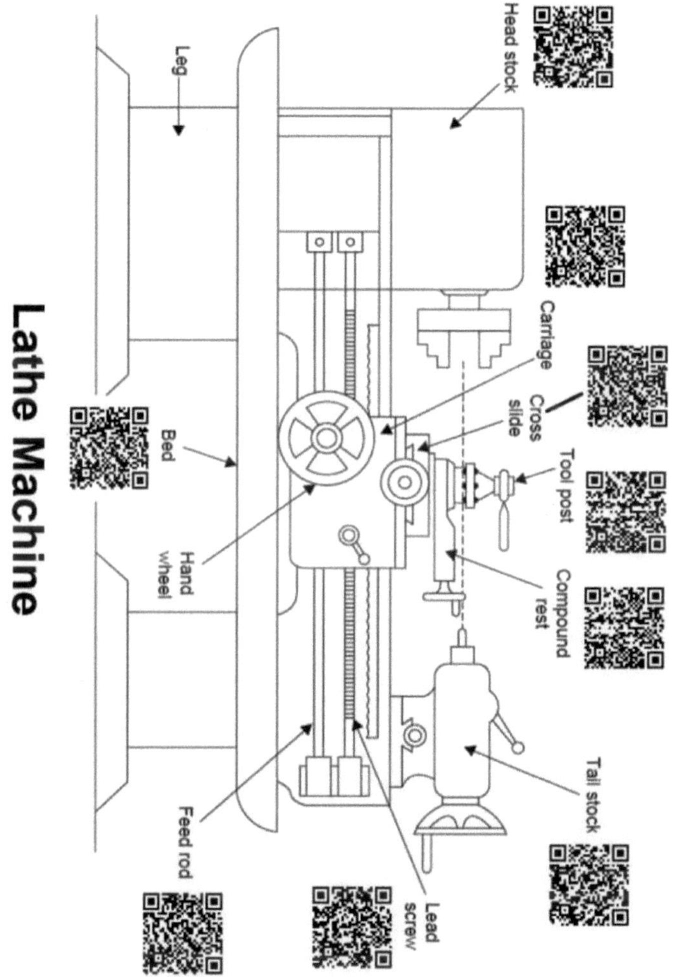
Lathe Machine
Head stock
Leg
Carriage
Cross slide
Tool post
Compound rest
Bed
Hand wheel
Tail stock
Feed rod
Lead screw

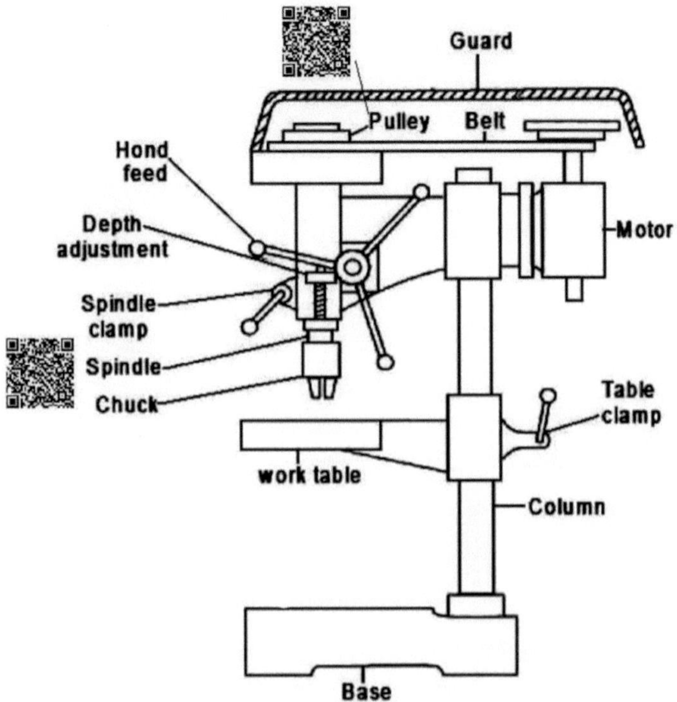

Piller Drilling Machine

Bench Grinding Machine

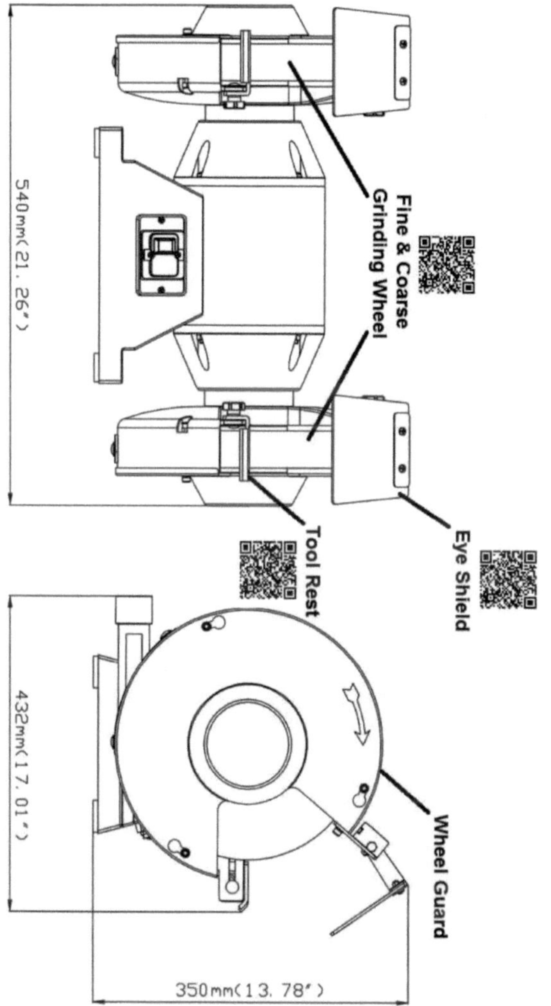

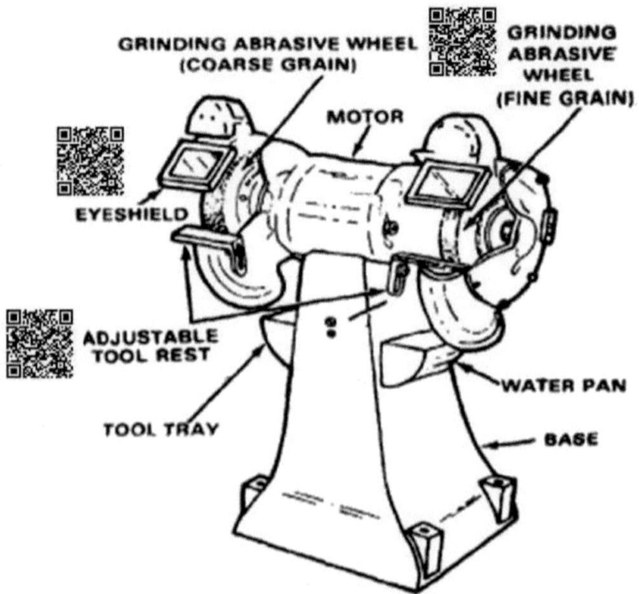

Pedastal Grinding Machine

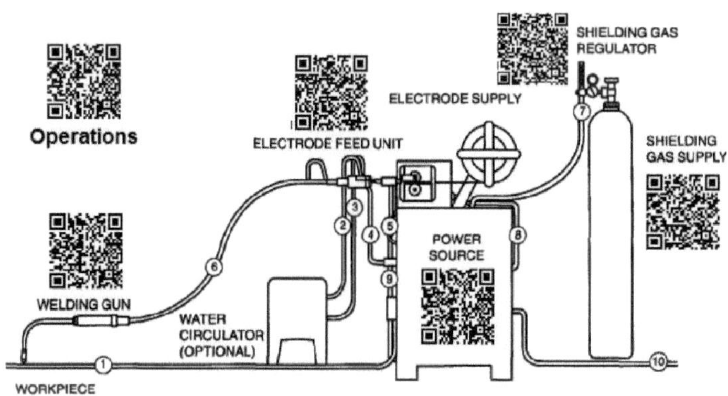

Gas Metal Arc Welding

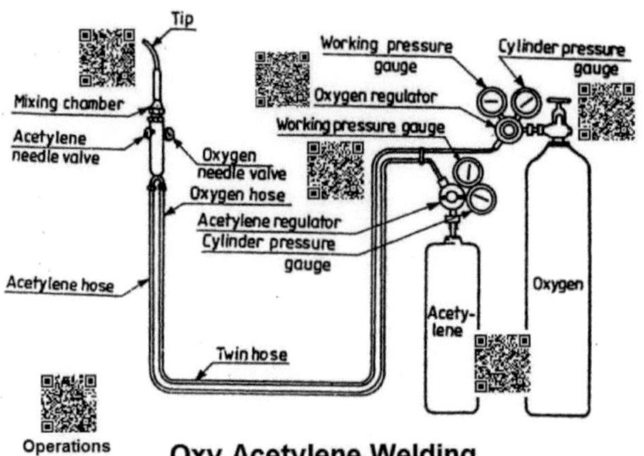

Oxy Acetylene Welding

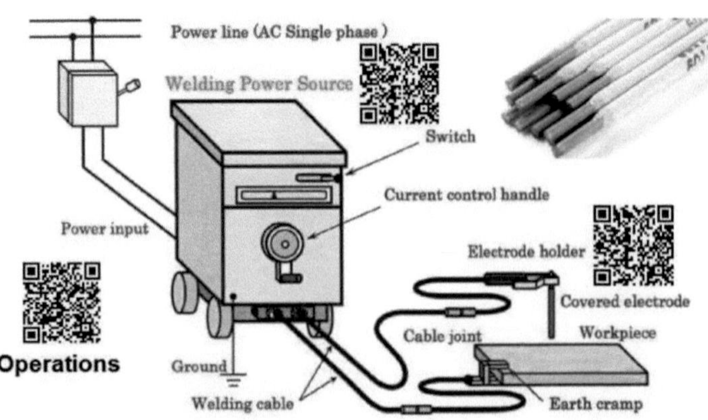

Shielded Metal Arc Welding

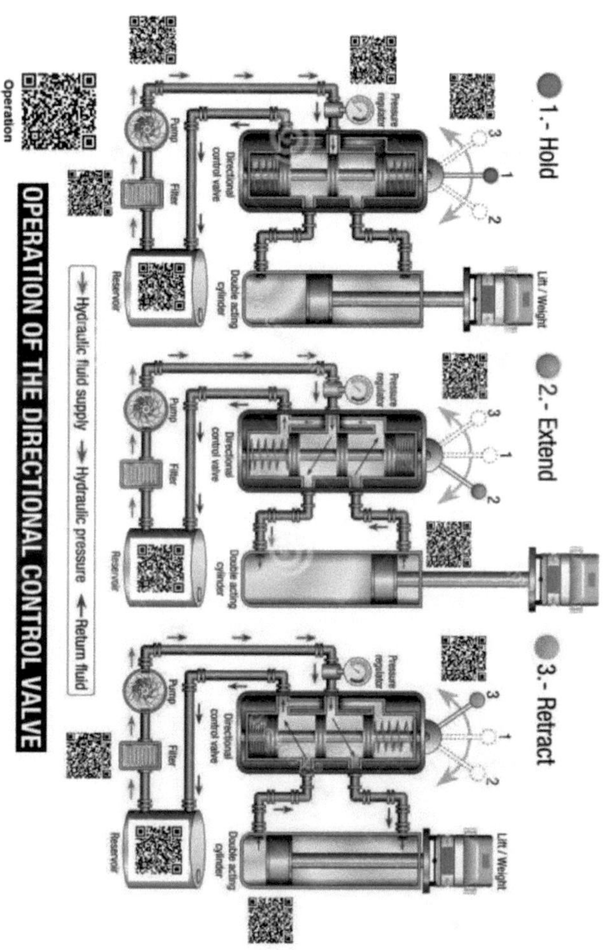
1.- Hold
2.- Extend
3.- Retract
Pressure regulator
Pump
Filter
Directional control valve
Reservoir
Double acting cylinder
Lift / Weight
Operation
Hydraulic fluid supply
Hydraulic pressure
Return fluid
OPERATION OF THE DIRECTIONAL CONTROL VALVE

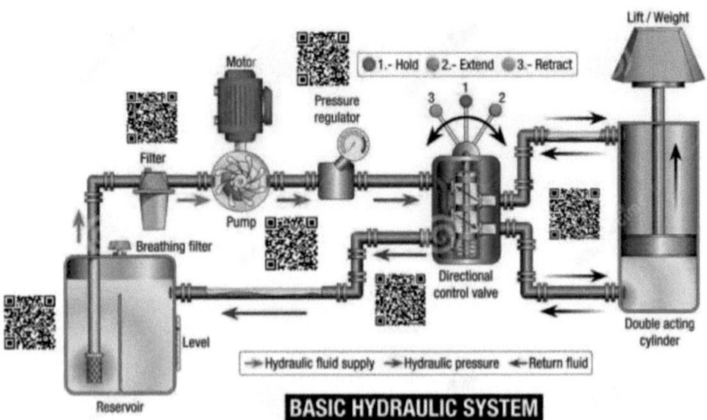

Direct Pressure Relief Valves

- The pressure relief valve provides protection against overload experienced by the actuators in a hydraulic system. One important function is to limit the force or torque produced by the hydraulic cylinders or motors.

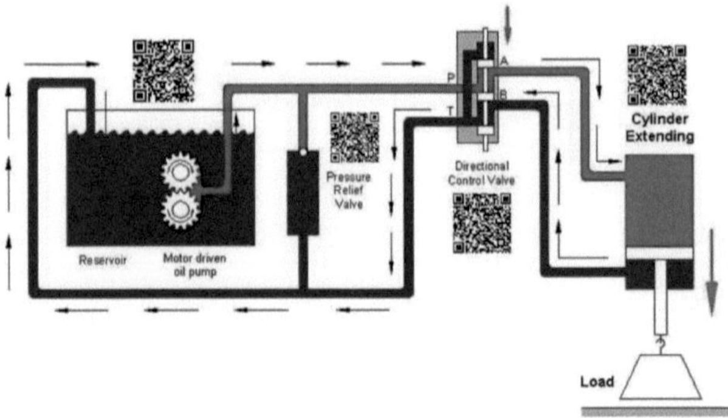

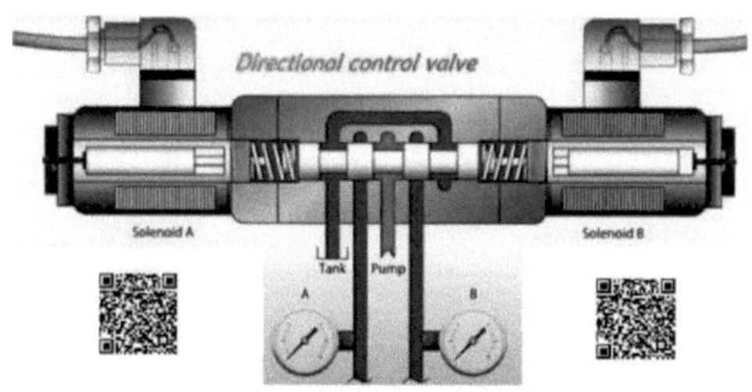
Directional control valve
Solenoid A
Solenoid B
Tank
Pump
A
B

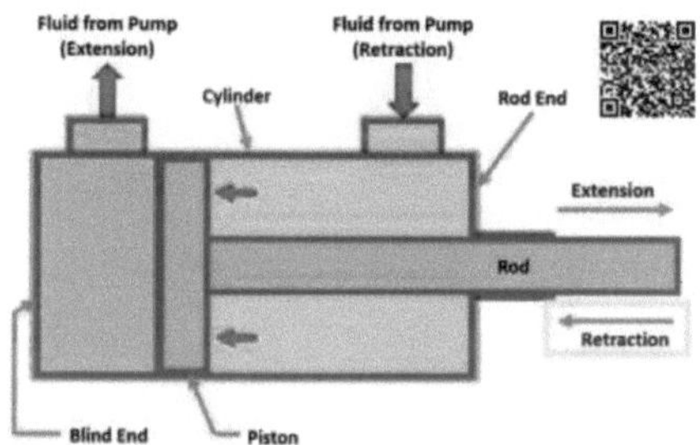
Double Acting, Single ended Cylinder
Fluid from Pump (Extension)
Fluid from Pump (Retraction)
Cylinder
Rod End
Extension
Rod
Retraction
Blind End
Piston

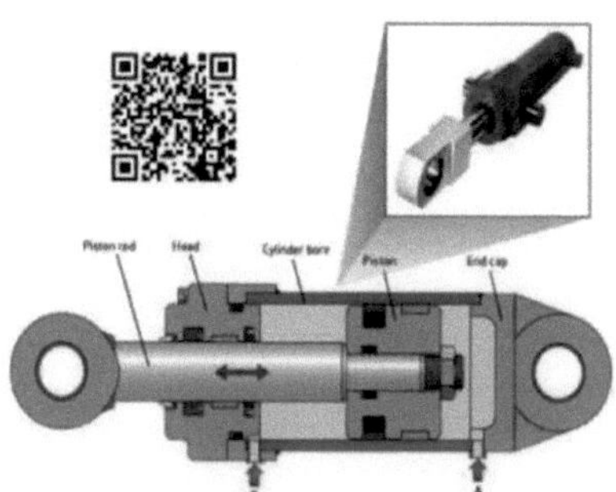
Hydraulic Cylinder

FLOW CONTROL VALVES

- A flow control valve can regulate the flow or pressure of the fluid.
- The fluid flow is controlled by varying area of the valve opening through which fluid passes.

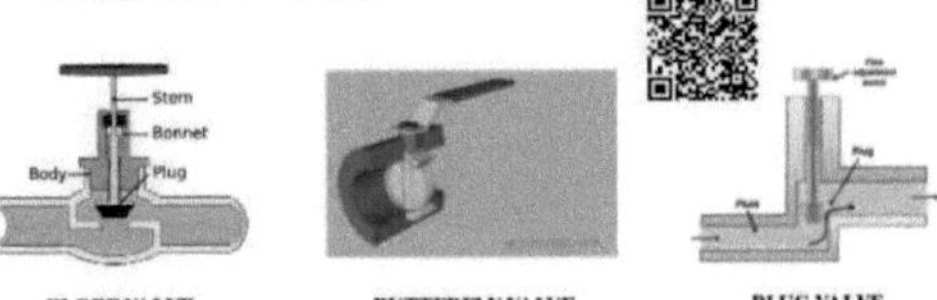

GLOBE VALVE　　BUTTERFLY VALVE　　PLUG VALVE

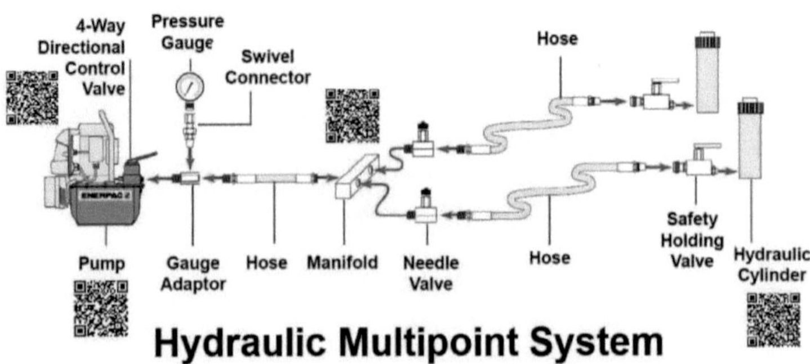

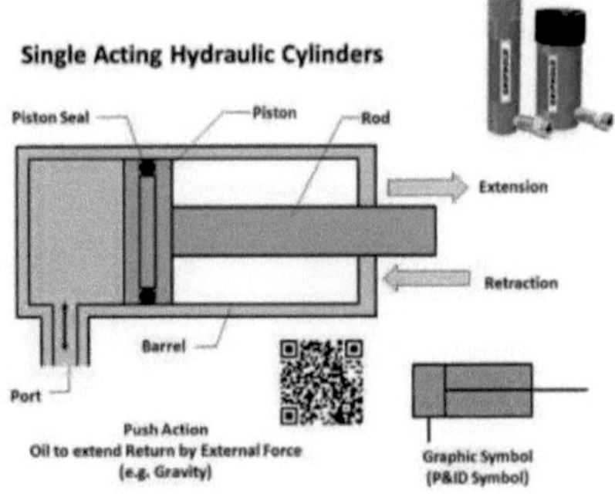

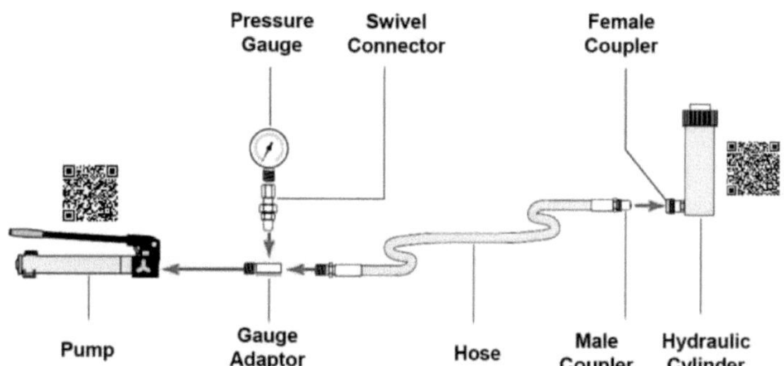

Hydraulic Single Point System

Types of Hydraulic Valves

- **Directional Control Valve:**

  Control the direction of flow of the hydraulic fluid to different lines in the circuit

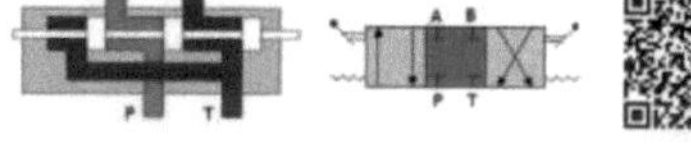

- **Flow Control Valves:**

  Control the amount of fluid flow in the circuit

- **Pressure Control Valves:**

  Control the pressure in different segments in the circuit

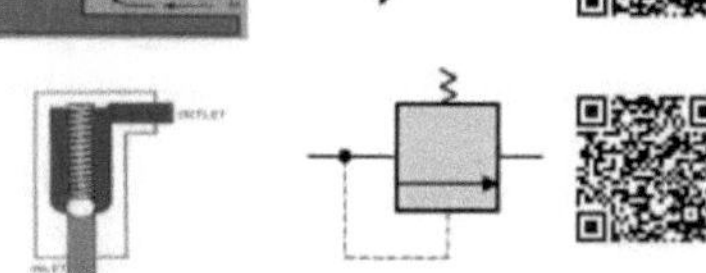

Hydraulic Valves - Parts and Components

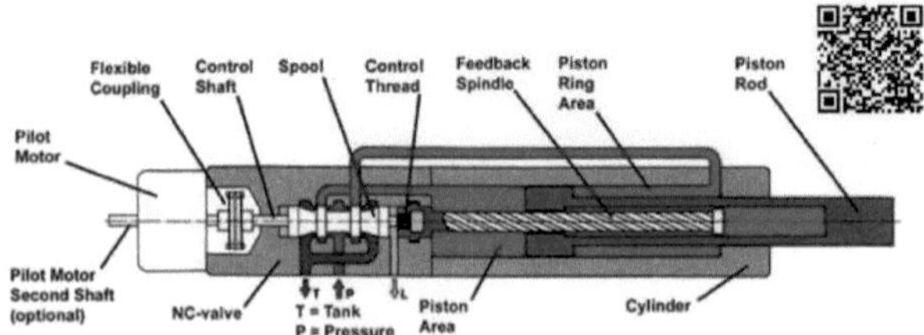

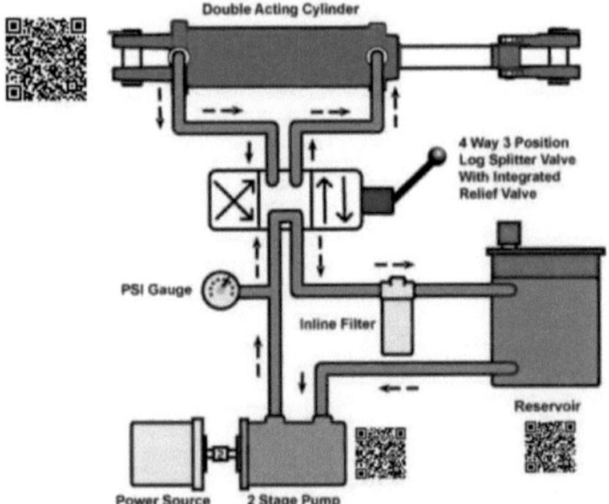

Hydraulic Double Acting Cylinder

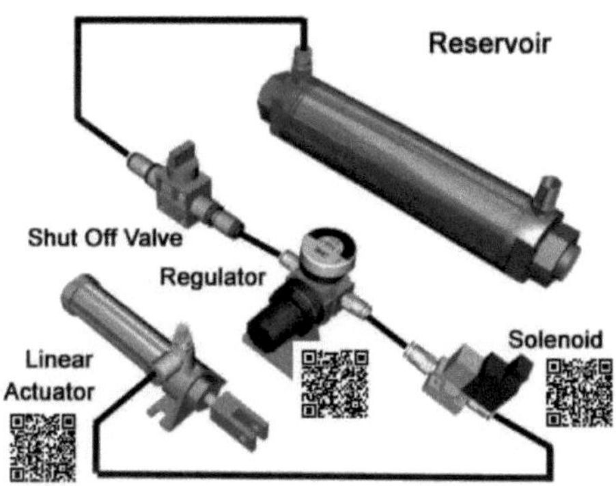

Pneumatic System

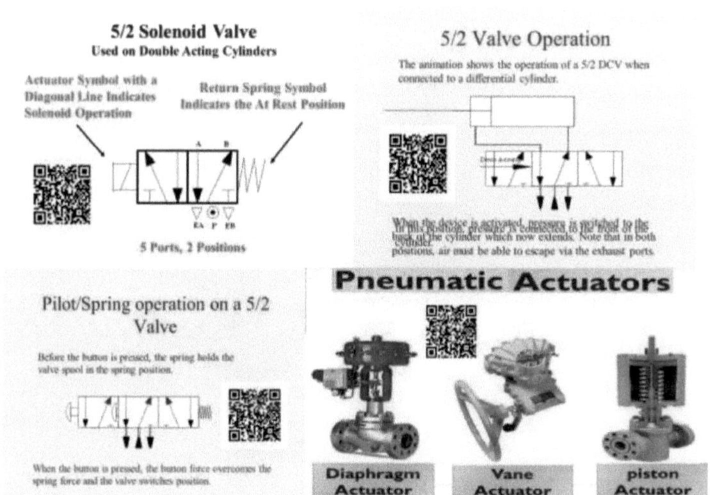

Pneumatic Control Valve

Pneumatic Control Valve Mechanisem

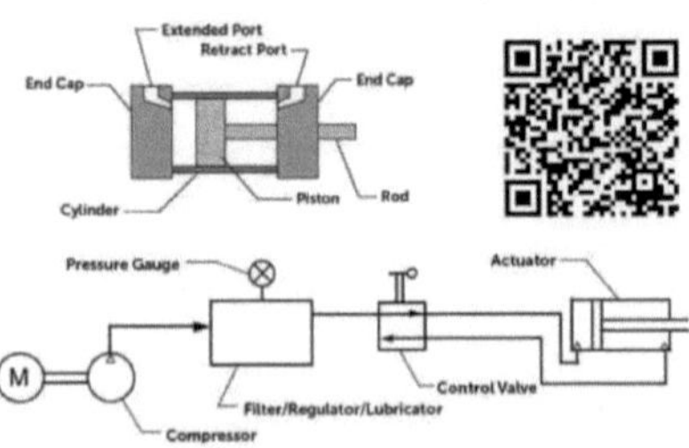

Pneumatic Cylinder System

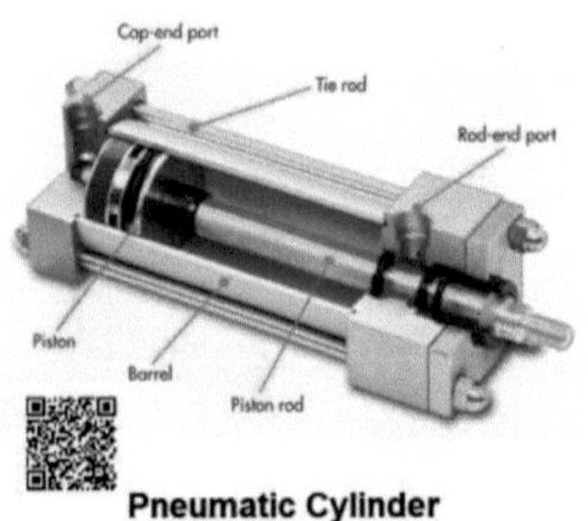

Pneumatic Cylinder

Pneumatic Cylinder

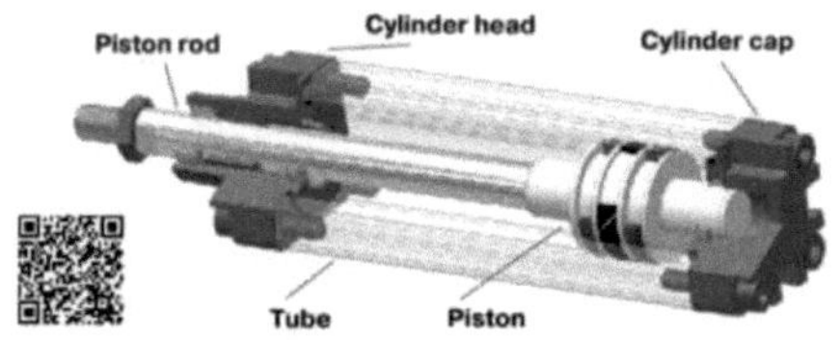

2-way, 2-position, normally closed direct-acting solenoid valve, spring return

4-way (5-port), 2-position, piloted solenoid valve, spring return

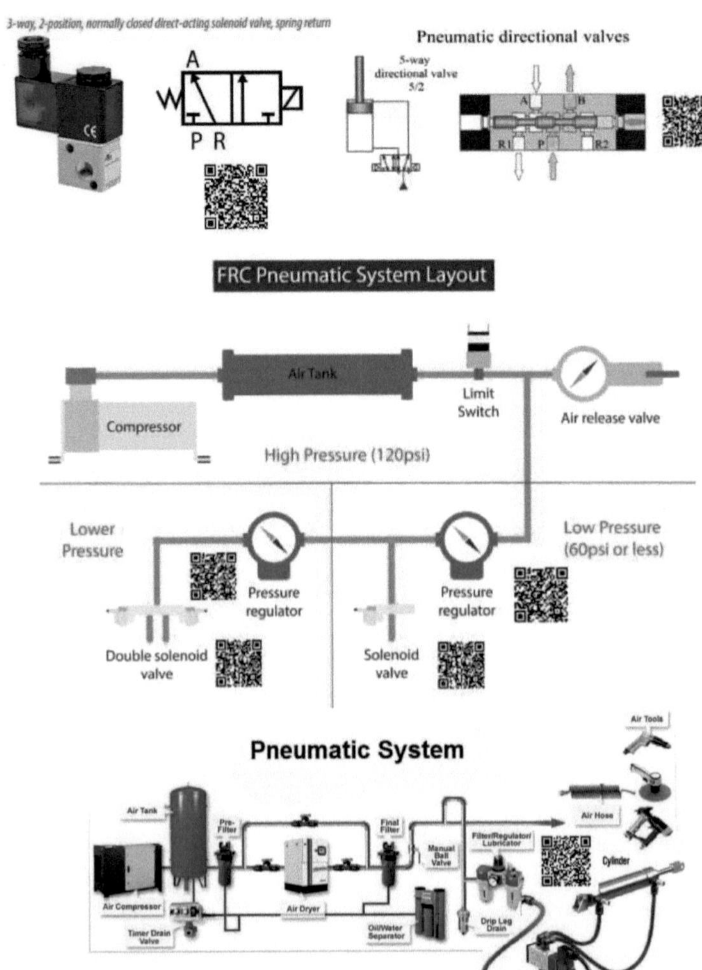
3-way, 2-position, normally closed direct-acting solenoid valve, spring return
A
P R
Pneumatic directional valves
5-way directional valve 5/2
A
B
R1
P
R2
FRC Pneumatic System Layout
Air Tank
Limit Switch
Air release valve
Compressor
High Pressure (120psi)
Lower Pressure
Pressure regulator
Pressure regulator
Low Pressure (60psi or less)
Double solenoid valve
Solenoid valve
Pneumatic System
Air Tools
Air Tank
Pre-Filter
Final Filter
Air Hose
Filter/Regulator/ Lubricator
Manual Ball Valve
Cylinder
Air Compressor
Air Dryer
Oil/Water Separator
Drip Leg Drain
Timer Drain Valve
Valve

CHAPTER TWO

Fitter Second Year MCQ

01] Used where bolt and threads are to be protected from damage.
A] Donald cap nut
B] Thumb nut
C] Hexagonal nut
D] Wing-nut

02] Used where frequent removal and fixing is required.
A] Donald cap nut
B] Thumb nut
C] Hexagonal nut
D] Wing-nut

03] Used in machine building and structure work.
A] Donald cap nut
B] Thumb nut
C] Hexagonal nut
D] Wing-nut

04] Used where frequent adjustments are to be made.
A] Donald cap nut
B] Thumb nut
C] Hexagonal nut
D] Wing-nut

05] Nylon inserts in the nut prevent loosening.
A] Locking plate
B] Wire lock
C] Self-locking nut
D] Sawn nut

06] A slot is cut halfway across the nut.
A] Locking plate
B] Wire lock

C] Self-locking nut

D] Sawn nut

07] Prevents slackening of two bolts.

A] Locking plate

B] Wire lock

C] Self-locking nut

D] Sawn nut

08] Prevents rotation of the top nut.

A] Lock-nut

B] Grooved nut

C] Self-locking nut

D] Sawn nut

09] Prevents loosening of nut by the use of a plate shaped to fit the nut.

A] Locking plate

B] Wire lock

C] Self-locking nut

D] Sawn nut

10] Hexagonal nut with the lower part made cylindrical and the recessed groove.

A] Lock-nut

B] Grooved nut

C] Self-locking nut

D] Sawn nut

11] Threading tools are checked for accuracy for the 60◦ angle by using a

A] Thread plug gauge

B] centre gauge

C] screw pitch gauge

D] tool angle gauge

12] The number of threads per inch can be checked with a

A] tool gauge

B] metric rule by counting

C] ring gauge

D] screw pitch gauge

screw pitch gauge

13] What is the angle of pipe thread?

A] 60°

B] 47‘/2°

C] 29°

D] 55°.

14] What is the use of pipe thread?

A] transmission

B] maintain pressure

C] airtight connections

D] none of the above.

15] What is the depth of the 2" pipe thread?

A] 0.5"

B] 0.640“

C] 0.335"

D] 0.580".

16] External Thread provide on Rod or Pipe , by Die and Cutting Tool is called ......

(A] Tapping

(B] Dieing

(C] Threading

(D] Grooving

Tap Die

17] The angle 0f lS thread (V shaped] is ----------

A] 29°

B] 47 1/4°

C] 50°

D] 60

18] ln which of the following methods, only external threads are made -------

A] Form tool mEthOd

B] Compound rest method

C] Tailstock offset method

D] Taper turning attachment method.

19] The surface joining the crest and the root of a thread is known as ----

A] Flank

B] Shank

C] Pitch surface

D] All Of these

20] Pitch of a two start thread is 4 mm. Then the lead of the thread is given by -----

A] 4mm

B] 2mm

C] 8mm

D] 6mm

21] The Gear ratio required for cutting a screw thread of 2.5 mm on a lathe having a lead screw pitch using single point cutting tool is ----

A] 1:2

B] 2:1

C] 1:1 mm

22] The depth of cut for M24 x 3 mm internal thread is

A] 0.5412 x 3
B] 0.6134 x 3
C] 0.5 x 3
D] 0.7 x 3
23] To cut 24 x 3 mm internal acme threads, the core diameter of the job is
A] 20.00 mm
B] 21.66 mm
C] 21.00 mm
D] 20.60 mm
24] The depth of cut for metric square threading is
A] 0.6 x P
B] 0.5 x P
C] 0.5412 x P
D] 0.6412 x P
25] To cut buttress thread, the depth of cut is
A] 0.5412 x P
B] 0.6 x P
C] 0.7 x P
D] 0.75 x P
26] What is template?
A] One of the cutting operation
B] One of the form turning
C] same figure of the job
D] one of the tool
27] Which purpose use template?
A] For marking & checking
B] for threading
C] for turning
D] for measuring
28] Which material is use for making template?
A] H.C.S. plate
B] Special tool steel
C] brass or copper
d] G.I. sheet or M.S. thin sheet
29] ---------------is used for checking shape of component
A] Template
B] Snap gauge

C] Instrument

D] Sine bar

30] For face copying......... Type template is used

A] Rounded

B] Plate type

C] Flat

D] Triangular

31] The accuracy of a taper is generally checked by means of......

A] taper gauges

B] gauge blocks

C] indicator and height gauge

32] External tapers are checked with

A] limit plug gauge

B] taper ring gauge

C]taper plug gauge

D] thread plug gauge.

33] To check the dimensional accuracy of identical components, a dial test indicator is set-for t 6 Size and used as a comparator. What will you use to set to the dial test indicator?

A] Dial test indicator

B] Teeter gauge

C] Slip gauge

D], surface gauge

34] Sine bar is used for

A] levelling the job for drilling

B] finding the angle of taper job

C] measuring diameter of holes

D] checking profile of thread.

Sine bar

35] Length of sine bar is the distance between

A] one end to another end of sine bar

B] diagonal cross length of the sine bar

C] centre to centre between rollers

D] outside to outside between rollers.

36] The size of a sine bar is specified by it's

A] weight

B] measurement of width

C] length

D] maximum angle of setting.

37]The purpose of providing a stopper at one end of the sine bar is for

A] easy handling

B] preventing the job from slipping .

C] supporting the slip gauge

D] using as a reference while setting.

38] A sine bar is made with four or five equally'spaced holes on its body. The purpose of these holes is to

A] Handle the sine bar easily

B] Reduce the weight of sin bar

C] Prevent distortion of the top surface of sine bar

D] Give good appearance to the sine bar

39] A sine bar is used for

A] Measuring the diameter of holes '

B] Finding the angle of a taper job

C] Leveling the job for drilling

D] Chuckin'g the profile of a thread

40] For measuring angles using the sine bar the angle framed according to the ratio between the height of slip gauge and the

A] Height of sine bar

B] Number slip gauge

C] Length of sine bar

D] Width of sine bar

41] -----------is used for checking angle within an accuracy of 1.

A] Gauge

B] Sine bar

C] Temple

D] Telescopic gauge

42] Centre line of the contact rollers and datum surface if the sine bar are

A] Same line' '

B] Parallel

C] Inclined

D] Perpendicular

43] The sine bar is made of -.

A] High carbon steel

B] Stabilized chromium steel '

C] High speed steel

D] Nicked steel

44] A sine bar with a length of l=200mm is used to check accurately the angle of a Work piece. The angle to be checked: 250 calculate the height 'h' of the slip gauges?

A] 84.54mm

B] 83.52mm

C] 81.81mm

D] 85.52mm

45] Which of the following statement is correct?'

A] Gauges are used to check the size

B] Template are used to chuck-the size

C] Gauges are used to measure the size

D] Gauges are used to check shape of component

46] At what standard temperature are the gauges kept in the section?

A] 100 C

B] 20° C

C] 100 F

D] 20° F

47] Which grade of slip gauge is generally used in workshop?

A] Grade 0

B] Grade l

C] Grade H

D] Grade 0

48] As per Indian Standards a special set gauge is used consisting of

A] 81 Pieces

B] 112 Pieces

C] 120 Pieces

D] 130 Pieces

49] The accuracy of reference gauge is

A] 0.05 mm

B] 0.01 mm

C] 0.001 .

D] 0.0001 mm

50] In case of ant burr on slip gauge, it should be removed by

A] Filling

B] Lapping

C] Scraping

D] Grinding

51] Hardness of slip gauge should be?

A] More than 63 HRC

B] 58 HRC

C] 55 HRC

D] 50 HRC

Slip gauge

52]------------- Slip gauge is used for Checking component within an accuracy of 0.01 mm.

A] Workshop gauge

B] Inspection gauge

C] Reference gauge

D] Ring gauge

53], ------------is used for checking accuracy of precision instrument.

A] Gauge block

B] Fader gauge

C] Sine bar

D] Plug gauge

54] Slip gauge are Cleaned before using to ensure accuracy. What medium will you use for this purpose.

A] Oil

B] Thinner

C] Carbon tetrachloride/ White petrol

D] Turpentine oil

55]To check the dimensional accuracy of identical components, a dial test indicator is set-for t 6 Size and used as a comparator. What will you use to set to the dial test indicator?

A] Dial test indicator

B] Teeter gauge

C] Slip gauge

D], surface gauge

Dial test indicator

56] which one of the following statement about Sine bar is not correct?

A] Uses tow precision rollers kept on either side

B] Made of the Chromium steel

C] The surface is lapped

D] The centrelines of the holes will be inclined to the top surface

57] A slip gauge is a ----------

A] Rectangular block

B] Square block

C] Cubic block

D] Cylindrical block

58] In 4th SERIES of slip gauge, which one of the following range is correct in set 46 pieces

A] 1.0 to 9.0 mm.

B] 1.001 101.009 mm

C] 1.01 to 1.09 mm

D]'1.1'to_-1.9mm

59] In 5th SERIES of slip gauge, which one Of the following range is correct in set 46 pieces –

A] 100to 100 mm ‘
B] 1.001 to 1.009 mm
C] 1.01 to 0.09mrn
D] 11 to 9mm

60] In 2NDS SERIES of slip gauge, which one of the following range IS correct in set of 45 pieces-

A] 1.0 to 9.0 mm
B] 1.001 to 1. 009 mm
C] 1.01 to 1.09 mm
D] 1.1 to 1.9mm

61] In 3RD SERIES of slip gauge, which one of the following range is correct in set 46 pieces –

A] 10.0 to 100 mm
B] 1.001 to 1.009 mm
C] 1.01 to 1.09 mm
D] 1.1 to 1.9 mm

62] In 1ST SERIES of slip gauge, which one of the following range is correct in set 46 pieces –

A] 0.001mm
B] 001mm
C] 0.1mm
D] 1.0mm

63] In 2ned SERIES of slip gauge, which one of the following STEP is correct in set of 46 pieces –

A] 0.001mm
B] 0.01 mm
C] 0.1 mm
D] 1-0 mm

64] In 3rd SERIES of slip gauge, which one of the following STEP Is correct in set 46 pieces

A] 0.001mm
B] 0.01mm
C] 0.1 mm
D] 1.0mm

65] In following which type of tip for cemented carbide treading tool?

A] For clamping on reject tool
B] with brazing on tool
C] With welding on tool

66] The number of threads per inch can be checked with a

A] tool gauge

B] metric rule by counting

C] ring gauge

D] screw pitch gauge

67] Telescopic gauges are used to measure holes and slots.

A] from 10 mm to 100 mm

B] from 12 mm to 152 mm

C] from 12.7 mm to 152.4 mm

D] none of the above.

Telescopic gauge

68] Small hole gauges are used to measure holes and slots.

A] below 10 mm

B] below 12.7 mm

C] below 20 mm

D] below 20.7 mm.

69] A set of number drill series consists of drills in the following ranges. Indicate the correct range

A] 1 to 40

B] 1 to 50

C] 1 to 80

D] 1 to 100

70] In the number drill series, the smallest drill size is...

A] 0.1 mm

B] 0.35 mm

C] 0.5 mm

D] 0.52 mm

71] In the number drill series, the largest drill size is...

A] 102 mm

B] 5.791 mm

C] 5.613 mm

D] 5.410 mm

72] In the letter drill series, the size of the drill 'A' is equal to ...

A] 13 mm

B] 6.08 mm

C] 6.045 mm

D] 5.944 mm

73] In the letter drill series, the largest drill size is equal to...

A] 10.33 mm

B] 10.490 mm

C] 12.01 mm

D] 15.00 mm

74] The feeler gauge is used for...

A] Checking surface roughness

B] Checking the redius of workpieces

C] Checking the gap between mating parts

D] Checking the accuracy of the hole locators

Feeler gauge

75] The purpose of relief grooves is to...

A] Maintain the required type of fit

B] Ensure contact between surfaces without any obstruction

C] Make for lubrication

D] Adjust the components for play

76] Generally gauges are made out of

A] nickel chromium

B] mild steel

C] cast steel

D] H.S.S.

77] Generally gauges are used for

A] mass production

B] measuring the components

C] individual component

D] checking the dimensional accuracy

78] A centre gauge is used to

A] check the pitch of the thread

B] set the tool at the correct centre height

C] check the fit of the thread

D] check the angle of the threading tool

Centre gauge

79] A metric centre gauge has an angle of

A] 55◦

B] 60◦

C] 47.5◦

D] 29◦

80] ln case of ant burr on slip gauge, it should be removed by

A] Filling

B] Lapping

C] Scraping

D] Grinding

81] The purpose for which lapping operation are carried out ---

A] To refine surface finish.

B] To improve quality of fit

C] To improve geometrical accuracy,

D] All the above

82] Lapping compound material is ----------

A] Sand stone

B] Diamond

C] Quartz

D] Corundum

83] When does the work piece get charged with the abrasive and cut the lap?

A] The work piece is harder than the lap

B] The work piece is softer than the lap

C] The lap is softer than the work piece

D] The lap is coarser than the work piece

84] The grooves are provided on the lapping plate for-----------..

A] Preventing distortion of the plate

B] Retaining lapping paste

C] Reducing friction

D] Collects the metal-chips

85] The following material is used for diamond lapping ....

A] H55

B] Copper ‘

C] Aluminium oxide,

D] High carbon steel

86] Which one of the following is a cold working process by which improvement of surface finish, dimensional accuracy and work hardening can be affected without removal of metal?

A] Burnishing

B] Honing

C] Lapping _

D] Super finishing

87] In the honing Process, the movement of the spindle is ---‘ ------------

A] Vertical and reciprocating

B] Reciprocating

C] Vertical

D] Horizontal and reciprocating

88] lt is the process carried out by using abrasive stick?

A] Lapping

B] Honing

C] Super finishing

89] This process is carried out in both hardened and unhardened state ------

A] Burnishing

B] Super finishing

C] Lapping

D] Honing

90] Honing process is preferred for -------------.

A] Finishing internal holes

B] Boring of carbides

C] Internal threads cutting '

D] External grinding

91] The range of surface roughness in Honing is in the range of --------

A] 0.9 to 5 microns

B] 0.1 to 5 microns

C] 0.13 to 1.25 microns

D] 0 to 100 microns

92] The productivity of honing Operation is

A] Less than the productivity of lapping Operation

B] More than the productivity of lapping operation

C] Equal to the productivity of lapping operation for the same work piece

D] None of these

93] Material For bearing lining.

A] Duralumin

B] Brass

C] Bronze

D] Babbit

94] Unbalanced load.

A] Bearing pinched in the housing.

B] Discolouration of bearing.

C] Spinning of the outer ring in the housing

D] Ball or Roller denting.

95] Housing warped.

A] Bearing pinched in the housing.

B] Discolouration of bearing.

C] <u>Spinning of the outer ring in the housing</u>

D] Ball or Roller denting.

96] Distorted shaft and other parts of the bearing assembly

A] Bearing pinched in the housing.

B] <u>Discolouration of bearing.</u>

C] Spinning of the outer ring in the housing

D] Ball or Roller denting.

97]Housing bore too large.

A] Bearing pinched in the housing.

B] Discolouration of bearing.

C] <u>Spinning of the outer ring in the housing</u>

D] Ball or Roller denting.

98] Incorrect method of mounting.

A] <u>Bearing pinched in the housing</u>.

B] Discolouration of bearing.

C] Spinning of the outer ring in the housing

D] Ball or Roller denting.

99] Housing bore out of round.

A] <u>Bearing pinched in the housing</u>.

B] Discolouration of bearing.

C] Spinning of the outer ring in the housing

D] Ball or Roller denting.

100] Prevents dust or grit entering into shaft bearings.

A] '0' ring seal

B] Radial lip seal

C] <u>Wiper seal</u>

D] Spring loaded seal

101] Heating plain carbon steel uniformly above the lower critical temperature, casuses the commencement Of the formation of solid solution called...

A] Ferrite

B] Pearlite

C] <u>Austenite</u>

D] Martensite

102] The process of heating and cooling for changing the structure of steel for obtaining the required properties is called...

A] Hardening

B] Heat treatment

C] Normalising

D] Tempering

103] The main purposes of annealing is

A] To increase the hardness

B] To increase the toughness

C] To improve machinability

D] To remove distoration

104] The process which helps in producing a fine grain for uniformity of structure and for improved mechanical properties is known as...

A] Tempering

B] Annealing

C] Hardening

D] Normalising

105] Which one of the following is an alloy of carbon and iron, in which carbon is in a combined state?

A] Steel

B] Wrought iron

C] Cast iron

D] Pig-iron

106] Carbon dissolved in the iron to form a solid solution is called

A] Cementite

B] Ferrite

C] Pearlite

D] Austenite

107] A chemical compound of carbon with iron is called...

A] Ferrite

B] Pearlite

C] Cementite

D] Austenite

108] Cementite and ferrite will together form a laminated structure in the steel which is called...

A] Martensite

B] Alloy steel

C] Austenite

D] Pearlite

109] Increase of carbon content in carbon steel beyond 0.83% results in proportional..

A] Reduction of elasticity

B] Increases in hardness

C] Increase in strength

D] Increase in ductility

110] Which one of the following is thermoplastics?

A] Phenolics

B] Aminos

C] Acrylic resin

D] Polyster resin

111] Which one of the following comes under thermosetting plastics category?

A] Cellulosics

B] Nylon

C] Epoxy

D] Polythene

112] The purpose of normalising steel is ....

(A] Remove induced stresses

(B] Improve machinability

(C] Soften the steel

(D] Increase the toughness and reduce brittleness

113] A carbon steel piece is heated just above 730°C maintained at that temperature for a few hours and then slowly cooled. What heat treatment process is carried out?

(A] Normalizing

(B] Case hardening

(C] Hardening

(D] Annealing

114]The toughness in a steel is increased and brittleness is decreased by a heat treatment operation called as......

A] Annealing

B] Normalizing

C] Tempering

D] Case hardening

115] Cyaniding and nitrating are two methods of........

A] Hardening

B] Case hardening

C] Tempering

D] Ammonising

116] The external surface of mild steel parts can be hardened by......

A] Tempering

B] Normalising

C] Hardening

D] Hardening

117]In nitrating process the NH3, gas is introduced at ....

A] 500°C 2 560°C

B] 600°C 3 650°C

C] 575°C 3 600°C

D] 650°C 3 700°

118]High speed steel is tempered at ....

A] 220°C 3 230°C

B] 280°C '6 400°C

C] 230°C '3 270°C

D] 550°C 3 600°C

119]Which one of the following process is used for surface hardening the of tool steel?

A] Carburising

B] Cyaniding

C] Induction hardening

D] Hardening

120]Lower critical temperature of higher" hon steel while hardening is.......

A] 960°C

B] 900°C

C] 723°C

D] 560°C

121]Approximate hardness of H.S.S. milling cutters is.........

A] 45HRCA

B] 52 HRC

C] 62 HRC

D] 75 HRC

122]What is the main purpose of annealing]

A] To improve machinability

B] To improve magnetism

C] To increase hardness

D] To increase toughness

123]Which one of the following is the solid early uprising material?

A] Charcoal

B] Petrol

C] Ammonia

D] Kerosene

124]While hardening after heating the steel to the required temperature it is held at that temperature as soaking time for normally]

A] 5 minutes for 10 mm thickness

B] 10 minutes for 5 mm thickness

C] 20 minutes for 2 mm thickness

D] 20 minutes for 2 mm thickness

125]Which one of the following quenching medium is used for hardening H.S.S. tool?

A] Water

B] Brine solution

C] Oil

D] Soda Water

126]The hardening temperature for high speed steel tool is......

A] 1250°C

B] 950°C

C] 850°C

D] 750°C

127]Which one of the following is the purpose of tempering a hardened steel.

A] To increase to toughness

B] To increase ductility

C] To increase hardness

D] To reduce hardness

128]While normalising the steel should be cooled....

A] In still air to room temperature

B] In oil

C] In forced air

D] In water

129]The process of increasing carbon percentage on the surface of low carbon steel is known as......

A] Hardening

B] Manning
C] Carburising
D] Tempering

130]The process of producing a component with tough and ductile core and a hard outer surface is known as......

A] Hardening
B] Case hardening
C] Tempering
D] Annealing

131]The process of heating steel to about 400C above the upper critical temperature and cooling it in still air to room temperature is known .....

A] Hardening
B] Annealing
C] Normalizing / grain running
D] Tempering

132] Which one of the following heat treatment process produces a scale-free surface on the component?

A] Flame Hardening
B] Case Hardening
C] Normalizing
D] Induction Hardening

133]The point angle of the indenter of vickcr hardness tester is......

A] 120°
B] 130°
C] 136°
D] 140°

134]Load range for B scale of Rockwell hardness tester ......

A] 5 kgf to 120 kgf
B] 10 kgf to 100 kgf
C] 10 kgf to 150 kgf
D] 100 kgf to 3000 kgf

135] The major load applied for Rockwell hardness testing method in '3' scale is 3....

A] 300 kgf
B] 15 kgf
C] 120 kgf
D] 100 kgf

136] The difference in reading between the minor and major load is taken into account' in.......

A] Brinell lmrdnless Test

B] Rockwell Hardness Test

C] Shore hardness Test

D] Vickers hardness Test

137] The process of heating and cooling to change the structure of steel for obtaining the required properties is called

A] Hardening

B] Normalizing

C] Heat treatment

D] Tempering

138] The main purpose of annealing is to

A] Increase the hardness

B] Increase the toughness

C] Improve machinability

D] Improve distortion

139] The purpose of normalizing steel is to -----------

A] Remove the induced Stress

B] Improve genes and reduce brittleness

C] Soften the metal

D] Increase the surface?

140] Which one of the following process is used for hardenmg the outer 5" Annealing

A] Hardening

B] Tempering

C] Case Hardening

D] Tear surface

141] The purpose of producing a component with tough and ductile core is known as......

A] Hardening

B] Case hardening

C] Tempering

D] annealing

142] Lower critical temperature of high carbon steel while hardening is ----------

A] 9600C

B] 900°C

c] 7230 c

D] 56O C

143] The process of Changing the structure and thus changing the properties by heating and 'cooling is known as --

A] Heat treatment

B] Alloying

C] Tempering

D] None of these

144] For refining the grain structure which one of the following heat treatment processes 'Is adopted.

A] Annealing

B] Hardening

C] Tempering

D] Normalising

145] Annealing is performed on iron and steel ---------

A] To remove internal stresses

B] To reduce hardness

C] To improve machinability

D] All of these

146] Which one of the following does not fall under the stages of heat treatment?

A] Heating

B] Cleaning

C] Quenching

D] Soaking

147] In following which type of tip for cemented carbide threading tool?

A] For clamping on reject tool

B] with brazing on tool

C] With welding on tool

D] With soldering on tool

148] The tip of a cemented carbide threading tool is

A] brazed

B] welded

C] soldered

D] clamped to the shank

149] Soft soldering is done

A] below 450◦ C

B] above 450◦C

C] at 900◦C

D] above 1000◦C

150] Brazing is done

A] at 1900◦C

B] above 450◦C

C] at 1000◦C

D] below 450◦C

151] A brazed joint is

A] weaker than a soldered joint

B] stronger than a solder join

C] stronger than a welded joint

D] weaker than a silver soldered joint

152] What is template?

A] One of the cutting operation

B] One of the form turning

C] same figure of the job

D] one of the tool

153] Which purpose use template?

A] For marking & checking

B] for threading

C] for turning

D] for measuring

154] Which material is use for making template?

A] H.C.S. plate

B] Special tool steel

C] brass or copper

d] G.I. sheet or M.S. thin sheet

155] ---------------is used for checking shape of component

A] Template

B] Snap gauge

C] Instrument

D] Sine bar

156] The jig bush used for drilling and reaming of a hole is...?

A] Press fit bush

B] Liner bush

C] Slip renewable bush

D] Fixed renewable bush

157] The following given which device is used for holding job & guide for toll while working?

A] Gauge

B] Housing

C] Jig

D] Fixture

Jig

158] The following given device which one for used clamping job only?

A] Jig

B] Fixture

C] Housing

D] Gauge

159] While fabricated by welding job which device is used for holding fixed or revolving if necessary up to 360°C of welding job?

A] Gauge

b] Template

C] Jig

D] Fixture

Fixture

160] The main things of drilling jig its not clamping with machine table which reason is correct given following?

A] it is strong for operation

B] it is easy for operation

C] many different size holes produce by different setting while drilling on job

D] for this device has lot of time

161] Following which locations is most usefull for round shape job location?

A] pin type locator

B] wedge type locator

C] vee locator

D] adjustable stop locators

162] Following which reason is correct for using bushing in drilling jigs?

A] easy for drilling

B] for fixed drill hole size

C] for accurate drilling operation

D] for given better finish drilling hole

163] The metal for manufacturing jig bush is...?

A] mild steel

B] cast iron

C] cast steel

D] tool steel

164] Given following bush which busing used for locating renewable bushing?

A] press fit bushing

B] linear bushing

C] special bushing

D] knurd bushing

165] jig has tolerance..?

A] five present of job tolerance

B] ten percent of job tolerance

C] 20% to 50% of job tolerance

D] 100% of job tolerance

166] Following which jig is use for location from bore?

A] plate jig

B] solid jig

C] post jig

D] box jig

167] Following which jig having drill plate?

A] solid jig

B] plate jig

C] box jig

D] table jig

168] Following which locator is used for internal diameter location?

A] solid saports

B] Pin type locator

C] Vee locator

D] nest locator

169] Drm jig bushing-are generally hardened to ------------.

A] Mild steel

B] Cast iron

C] Cast steel

D] Tooi steel

170] Jigs is device which -------------

A] Locate the work piece

B] Holding and supporting the work piece

C] Guide the cutting tool

D] Does all the above

171] Which among the following jigs is used forllocation from a bore?

A] Plate jig

B] Solid jig

C] Post jig

D] Box jig

172] Fixture is a production device which -----------.

A] Holds and locate the work piece

B] Holds the piece

C] Chats the work piece,

D] Neither holds nor. Locates the-work piece

173] Which one of the following is used to guide tool and hold the job in mass production? '

A] Gauge.

B] Housing

C] Fixture

D] Jig

174] Which among the following is the purpose for proi/iding bushing in a drill jig?

A] For locating accurately and guiding the drill for precise drilling operation

B] For determining the size of the hole to be drilled

C] For easy drilling

D] For getting good finished surface in the drilled holes

175] Drill jig are used for? _

A] Drill operations only.

B] Clamping the job for drilling

C] Drilling, Reaming, Tapping and other operations

D] Guiding the tools only

176] Which one of the following jigs consists of drill plate, which rests on the component to be drilled? . . . .

A] Solid jig .

B] Plate jig .

C] Box jig

D] Trunnion jig

177] Jig is a device which -----------

A] Locates the work piece .

B] Hold and supports the work piece and guides tool

C] Guides the cutting tool

D] Hold the cutting tool .

178] Drill jig are used for ....

A] Drilling, reaming, tapping and other allied operations

B] Drilling operations only

C] Clamping the job when drilling

D] Guiding the tool only

179] Fixture is a production device which---------: -----

A] holds the work piece '

B] Locate the work piece

C] Holds and locates the work piece

D] Neither holds nor locates the work piece

180] Purpose of the Box Jig is to

A] Hold the job and guide the tool to produce internal threads

B] To produce many inclined holes

C] To produce many straight holes

D] None of these

181] Jigs and fixtures are --------.

A] Machining tools

B] Precision tools

C] Both (a] & (b]

D] None of these

182] 'How jig are in terms of weight compared to fixtures?

A] Jigs are lighter than fixtures

B] Jigs are heavier than fixtures

C] jigs are equal in weight to fixtures for same operation

D] None of these

183] Which fixtures are used for machining parts which musthav-e machined details evenw spaced?

A] Profile fixtures

B] Duplex fixtures

C] Indexing fixtures

D] None of these

184] G.l. pipes are provided externally with

A] no threads

B] parallel threads

C] tapered threads

D] neither parallel nor tapered threads.

Thread

185] in the pipe assembly, the hemp packing is used

A] for easy engagement

B] to fill the gap between threads

C] to avoid leakage

D] to get tight fitting.

186]The sealing compound shall be applied on the pipe threads

A] before hemp packing

B] after hemp packing

C] before and after temp packing

D] none of the above.

187] Used on finished tubular wrench surfaces to avoid marking.

A Stillson pipe

B] Chain wrench

C] Strap wrench

D] Footprint wrench

188] Used for gripping and turning pipes and round stocks in confined places.

A] Stillson pipe

B] Chain wrench

C] Strap wrench

D] Footprint wrench

189] Used for holding iarge diameter pipes.

A] Stillson pipe

B] Chain wrench

C] Strap wrench

D] Footprint wrench

190] Used for gripping and turning pipes,tubes and cylindricai rods.

A] Stillson pipe

B] Chain wrench

C] Strap wrench

D] Footprint wrench

191] Secures rope to small pipe or rim.

A] Slip knot

B] Bowline knot

C] Square knot

D] Sheep shank knot.

192] It can be folded and carried to any place. Similar to the quick releasing type pipe vice.

A Portable folding pipe vice

B] Chain pipe vice

C] Pipe vice

D] None of above

193] Used to hold pipes more than 63mm to 200mm diameter.

A] Portable folding pipe vice

B] Chain pipe vice

C] Pipe vice

D] None of above

194] Used for quick holding and locating pipes. Used to hold pipes up to 63mm diameter.

A] Portable folding pipe vice

B] Chain pipe vice

C] Pipe vice

D] None of above

195] Provides deviation of 90°

A] Plug

B] Elbow

C] Bend

D] Reducer 'T' branczh

196] Provides change of direction with a long radius at right angle.

A] Plug

B] Elbow

C] Bend

D] Reducer 'T' branczh

197] Used for closing a line which has an internal thread.

A] Plug

B] Elbow

C] Bend

D] Reducer 'T' branczh

198] Provides deviation of'45°

A] Bend

B] Reducer 'T' branczh

C] Elbow

D] Tee piece

199] Provides outlet at right angles to the run.

A] Bend

B] Reducer 'T' branczh

C] Elbow

D] Tee piece

200] Used where a change in ' pipe diameter is required.

A] Bend

B] Reducer 'T' branczh

C] Elbow

D] Tee piece

201] Selection of a former depends on the

A] <u>outside diameter of the pipe</u>

B] wall thickness of the pipe

C] bore diameter of the pipe

D] all the above.

202] A branch type hand operated pipe bending machine is used to bend

A] P.V.C.pipes

B] onduit pipes

C] <u>G.I.pipes</u>

D] copper pipes.

203] The inner formers of a hydraulic pipe bending machine are able to bend pipes up to a diameter of

A] 40mm

B] 100mm

C] 20mm

D] <u>75mm</u>

204] The included angle of a pipe thread is

A] 60°

B] 47°

C] <u>55°</u>

D] 45°

205] G.l.pipes are available in a standard length of

A] 5 metres

B] 18"

C] <u>6 metres</u>

D] 16 feet.

206] The standard pipe fittings are provided with threads conforming with

A] BA

B] BSW

C] <u>BSP</u>

D] Metric.

207] The external threads on G.l.pipes are out easily

A] by tap sets

<u>B] dies and die stocks</u>

C] centre lathes

D] thread rollers.

208] Water flowing from tap even when firmly closed.

A] Spindle bent.
B] Defective washer.
C] Valve on the spindle loose.
D] Spindle thread worn-out.
209] Tap hard to turn on and off.
A] Spindle bent.
B] Defective washer.
C] Valve on the spindle loose.
D] Spindle thread worn-out.
210] Loud noise in the tap when turned on.
A] Spindle bent.
B] Defective washer.
C] Valve on the spindle loose.
D] Spindle thread worn-out.
211] G.l. pipes are provided externally with
A] no threads
B] parallel threads
C] tapered threads
D] neither parallel nor tapered threads.
212] in the pipe assembly, the hemp packing is used
A] for easy engagement
B] to fill the gap between threads
C] to avoid leakage
D] to get tight fitting.
213] The sealing compound shall be applied on the pipe threads
A] before hemp packing
B] after hemp packing
C] before and after temp packing
D] none of the above.
214] To put off"Class B" fire, the types of fire extinguisher used is ....
A] dry power
B] Carbon dioxide
C] Jet of water
D] Foam type

fire extinguisher

215] Which type of fire extinguisher is used to put off general fire?

A] Water type Extinguisher

B] Foam type Extinguisher

C] Dry chemical powder Extinguisher

D] Carbon dioxide (C02] Extinguisher

216] lt is a reverse process of metal plating.

A] Electro~discharge machining

B] Electrochemical machining

C] Ultrasonic machining

D] Wire cut EDM

217] lt is used for making narrow slots and detailed internal features using sparks developed between a thin slender electrode and the work piece.

A] Electro~discharge machining

B] Electrochemical machining

C] Ultrasonic machining

D] Wire cut EDM

218] Electrodes made from metal or carbon in the shape of the piece point are used.

A] Electro~discharge machining

B] Electrochemical machining

C] Ultrasonic machining

D] Wire cut EDM

219] High frequency sound is used as the force with which to propel abrasive particles against the work piece.

A] Electro~discharge machining

B] Electrochemical machining

C] Ultrasonic machining

D] Wire cut EDM

220] Any intricate shape can be made without producing any chip, using electrodes made in the shape of the piece part.

A] Electro~discharge machining

B] Electrochemical machining

C] Ultrasonic machining

D] Wire cut EDM

221] For transmitting very low torque.

A] Feather key

B] Gib head key

C] Woodruff key

D] Saddle key

222] Profile of key tends to weaken the shaft.

A] Feather key

B] Gib head key

C] Woodruff key

D] Saddle key

223] For transmitting unidirectional torque.

A] Feather key

B] Gib head key

C] Woodruff key

D] Saddle key

224] For transmitting heavy torque.

A] Feather key

B] Gib head key

C] Woodruff key

D] Saddle key

225] For transmitting very high torque of the impact type in both directions of rotation.

A] Gib head key

B] Woodruff key

C] Saddle key

D] Tangential key

226] Permits sliding or axial movement of the mat« ing piece on the shaft.

A] Feather key

B] Gib head key
C] Woodruff key
D] Saddle key
227] Can be withdrawn easily.
A] Feather key
B] Gib head key
C] Woodruff key
D] Saddle key
228] Material For bearing lining.
A] Duralumin
B] Brass
C] Bronze
D] Babbit
229] Material For stressed components in aircraft.
A] Duralumin
B] Brass
C] Bronze
D] Babbit
230] Material For car radiator core.
A] Duralumin
B] Brass
C] Bronze
D] Babbit
231] Material For brazing rods.
A] Duralumin
B] Brass
C] Bronze
D] Babbit
232] For severe deep drawing.
A] Copper
B] Muntz metal
C] Cartridge brass
D] Lead
233] Useful for hot stamping.
A] Copper
B] Muntz metal
C] Cartridge brass
D] Lead

234] For coating on roofing sheets.

A] Cartridge brass

B] Lead

C] Cast phosphorbronze

D] Zinc

235] For coating in food l containers.

A] Lead

B] Cast phosphorbronze

C] Zinc

D] Tin

236] For preparation of primer paint.

A] Copper

B] Muntz metal

C] Cartridge brass

D] Lead

237] For protection against salt water corrosion.

A] Cartridge brass

B] Lead

C] Cast phosphorbronze

D] Zinc

238] If Less tension in belt

A] Belt slips.

B] Belt is damaged.

C] Belt whips.

D] Belt squeals.

239] If Misalignment in belt

A] Belt slips.

B] Belt is damaged.

C] Belt whips.

D] Belt squeals.

240] If Pulsating load on belt

A] Belt slips.

B] Belt is damaged.

C] Belt whips.

D] Belt squeals.

241] If High starting torque on pully

A] Belt slips.
B] Belt is damaged.
C] Belt whips.
D] Belt squeals.

242] If Shock load on belt
A] Belt slips.
B] Belt is damaged.
C] Belt whips.
D] Belt squeals.
243] If Centre distance between pulleys is more.
A] Belt slips.
B] Belt is damaged.
C] Belt whips.
D] Belt squeals.
244] This allows positive transmission of power at larger angles.
A] Slip type coupling
B] Plate coupling
C] Clamp coupling
D] Universal coupling
245] This disengages automatically when the. torque is higher than the friction generated by the spring and jaw.
A] Slip type coupling
B]] Plate coupling
C] Clamp coupling
D] Universal coupling
246] This can be used only when the shafts are in perfect alignment.
A] Slip type coupling
B] Plate coupling
C] Clamp coupling
D] Universal coupling
247] This does not permit any axial movement of the shafts.
A] Slip type coupling
B] Plate coupling
C] Clamp coupling
D] Universal coupling
248] This is used in automobile vehicles.
A] Slip type coupling

B] Plate coupling

C] Clamp coupling

D] Universal coupling

249] ------------ grooves are most commonly found on pulleys driven by V belts

A] 'V' Shaped

B] Slotted Shaped.

C] Square Shaped

D] Round Shaped

250] The hull gear wheel is driven

A] by a shaft

B] by a pinion

C] by sliding block.

D] None of above

251] Rotary motion is converted into reciprocating motion by means of the

A] rocker arm and bull gear

B] rack and pinion

C] worm and worm gear

D] None of above

252] in one complete revolution of the bull gear wheel the ram gets

A] one reverse stroke

B] one forward and one reverse stroke

C] one forward stroke.

D] None of above

253] The return stroke takes

A] less time than the forward stroke

B] more time than the forward stroke

C] equal time as the forward stroke.

D] None of above

254] Lubricant is necessary to ....

A] run the machine smoothly taking least load

B] Run the machine quickly

C] Stop the machine immediately

D] Produce work piece of greater accuracy

255] Extreme pressure additive (EPA] is mixed with cutting fluid for improving its power of.

A] Cooling

B] Lubrication

D] Production of the machined surface

C] Cleaning of cutting zone

256] The main purpose for using a lubricant in machine tools is to ------

A] Cool down the making parts

B] Prevent machine tool from heating

C] Wet the making parts for close contact

D] Minimize the friction between the making parts

257] Preventive maintenance is ....

A] The maintenance involves the use of sensitive instruments

B] The maintenance generally performed by operator himself

C] The work carried only when machine break down

D] plan to minimize the unforeseen break down

258] What is a break down maintenance?

A] Maintenance to minimize the unforeseen breakdown

B] Maintenance generally performed by operator himself

C] Maintenance involves replacement of worn out parts

D] Repairs work carried only when machine breakdown

259] The Routine Maintenance is ---------

A] it is planned maintenance to minimize the unforeseen breakdown

B] This type of maintenance involves the use of sensitive instrument

C] It is repair work carried only when machine breakdowns

D] This types of maintenance is generally performed by operator himself

260] Which one of the following is the advantage of pneumatic system?

A] For low cost layout

B] For increasing the rate of production

C] For better working environment

261] Which is not the property of hydraulic fluid used in grinding machine?

A] it must not control or absorb air

B] it must not cause corrosion of the moving parts

C] Should have adequate viscosity

D] it must vaporize at the operating temperature

262] Filling up of the gap be» tween the bottom of the machine and the top of the floor or foundation block.

A] Wooden forms

B] Foundation bolts

C] Grouting

D] Template

263] Used to prevent any movement when the concrete is poured.

A] Wooden forms

B] Foundation bolts

C] Grouting

D] Template

264] Used to hold down the machine firmly on the foundation to prevent it from moving.

A] Wooden forms

B] Foundation bolts

C] Grouting

D] Template

265] Wooden patterns which represents the base of the machine and support bolts over the excavation.

A] Wooden forms

B] Foundation bolts

C] Grouting

D] Template

266] After placing this in the excavation it is firmly braced from the outside to withstand the pressure of concrete.

A] Wooden forms

B] Foundation bolts

C] Grouting

D] Template

267] Used to check the level of the machine

A] Crowbar

B] Spirit level

C] Levelling jacks

D] Wedge

268] Driven into the gap between the machine base and floor for levelling.

A] Crowbar

B] Spirit level

C] Levelling jacks

D] Wedge

269] Used for lifting the machine.

A] Crowbar

B] Spirit level

C] Levelling jacks

D] Wedge

270] This is minimised by using anti-vibration pads.

A] Spirit level

B] Levelling jacks

C] Wedge

D] Vibration

271] Periodic re-levelling can be done quickly it this is used.

A] Crowbar

B] Spirit level

C] Levelling jacks

D] Wedge

183] Most hydraulic circuits:

a) Operate from a central hydraulic power unit

b) Use air-over-oil power units

c) Have a dedicated power unit

d) Does not have dedicated power unit

184] Hydraulic and pneumatic circuits:

a) Perform the same way for all functions

b) Perform differently for all functions

c) Perform the same with some exceptions

d) Does not perform all the functions

185] The lubricator in a pneumatic circuit is the:

a) First element in line

b) Second element in line

c) Last element in line

d) Third element in line

186] When comparing first cost of hydraulic systems to pneumatic systems, generally they are:

a) More expensive to purchase

b) Less expensive to purchase

c) Cost is same

d) Cost is not required

187] When comparing operating cost of hydraulic systems to pneumatic systems, generally they are.

a) More expensive to operate

b) Less expensive to operate

c) Cost is same to operate

d) Cost is not required

188] The most common hydraulic fluid is:

a) Mineral oil

b) Synthetic fluid

c) Water

d) Gel

189) Which fluid is used in hydraulic power systems?

a] water

b] oil

c] non-compressible fluid

d] all of the above

190) Pressure of 1 bar is equal to

a] 14]5 psi

b] 145 psi

c] 12]5 psi

d] 145 x 10-6 psi

191) What effect does overloading have on fluid power and electrical systems?

a] electrical components get damaged in electrical systems

b] fluid power system stops working without damaging the components

c] both a] and b]

d] none of the above

192) How is power transmitted in fluid power systems?

a] power is transmitted instantaneously

b] power is transmitted gradually

c] both a] and b]

d] none of the above

193) Generally liquids are non-compressible but when a large pressure of 70 bar is applied, petroleum oil can be compressed up to

a] 0]5% of its original volume

b] 1% of its original volume

c] 5% of its original volume

d] none of the above

194) The resistance offered to the flow of fluid inside a piston develops into

a] pressure

b] force

c] stress

d] all of the above

195) At low pressures, liquids are

a] compressible

b] non-compressible

c] unpredictable

196) In hydraulic systems,

a] the mechanical energy is transferred to the oil and then converted into mechanical energy

b] the electrical energy is transferred to the oil and then converted into mechanical energy

c] the mechanical energy is transferred to the oil and converted into electrical energy

d] none of the above

197) Which of the following is used as a component in hydraulic power unit?

a] pressure gauge

b] filler gauge

c] valve

d] reservoir

198) Rotary motion in a hydraulic power unit is achieved by using

a] hydraulic cylinder

b] pneumatic cylinder

c] both hydraulic and pneumatic cylinder

d] none of the above

199) What is the relation between speed and flow rate for fixed displacement vane pump?

a] flow rate increases with increase in speed of rotor

b] flow rate decreases with increase in speed of rotor

c] flow rate is constant and does not change with change in speed

d] none of the above

200) In fixed displacement vane pump,

a] flow rate decreases with increase in working pressure

b] flow rate increases with increase in working pressure

c] flow rate is constant and does not change with working pressure

d] none of the above

201) Which type of motion is transmitted by hydraulic actuators?

a] linear motion

b] rotary motion

c] both a] and b]
d] none of the above
202) What is the function of electric actuator?
a] converts electrical energy into mechanical torque
b] converts mechanical torque into electrical energy
c] converts mechanical energy into mechanical torque
d] none of the above
203) Which of the following is a hydraulic cylinder based on construction?
a] single acting cylinder
b] double acting cylinder
c] welded design cylinder
d] all of the above
204) Which energy is converted into mechanical energy by the hydraulic cylinders?
a] hydrostatic energy
b] hydrodynamic energy
c] electrical energy
d] none of the above
205) What is the advantage of using a single acting cylinder?
a] high cost and reliable
b] honing inside the inner surface of pump is not required
c] piston seals are not required
d] all of the above
206) What is the function of a flow control valve?
a] flow control valve changes the direction of oil flow
b] flow control valve can adjust the flow rate of hydraulic oil
c] both a] and b]
d] none of the above
207) What does the numbers in 4/2 valve mean?
a] 4 positions and 2 ways
b] 4 ways and 2 positions
c] none of the above
d] 3 ways 2 positions
208) Which type of solenoid has more chances of coil failure?
a] AC solenoid
b] DC solenoid
c] both AC and DC solenoids

d] none of the above

209) Which stage in two stage direction control valve is solenoid operated?

a] main stage direction control valve

b] pilot stage direction control valve

c] both stages in two stage direction control are solenoid operated

d] none of the above

210) Which of the following is a gas charged accumulator?

a] bladder type

b] spring loaded accumulator

c] weighted accumulator

d] all of the above

211) How is pressure of fluid under piston calculated in a weighted accumulator?

a] pressure of fluid = (weight added / piston area)

b] pressure of fluid = (piston area / weight added)

c] pressure of fluid = (weight added / piston force)

d] pressure of fluid = (piston force / weight added)

212) Which of the following gas is used in gas charged accumulator?

a] oxygen

b] nitrogen

c] carbon dioxide

d] all of the above

213) The relation for rapid change in pressure and volume adiabatically is given as

a] p0 v0 = p1 v1 = p2 v2

b] p0 v0 = p1 v1n = p2 v2n

c] p0 v0n = p1 v1n = p2 v2n

d] none of the above

214) Why is the pilot operated check valve used in clamping operation?

a] to reduce leakage in spool valve

b] to avoid decrease in pressure during clamping

c] *both a] and b]*

d] none of the above

215) Which area does the part shown below indicate?

a] rod area

b] full bore area

c] annulus area

d] none of the above

216) Which of the following statements is true?

a] Meter-in feed circuits have speed control in two directions

b] Standard block feed circuits have speed control in two directions

c] Tank line feed control systems have speed control only in one direction

d] all of the above

217) Leakage in rotary chucks can be compensated by

a] flow control valve

b] pilot operated check valve

c] accumulator

d] all of the above

218) Which valve is used to block the accumulator from the system for the purpose of safety?

a] pilot valve

b] needle valve

c] detent valve

d] all of the above

219) Which of the following systems generate more energy when used in industrial applications?

a] hydraulic systems

b] pneumatic systems

c] both systems generate same energy

d] cannot say

220) Which type of compressor requires a reservoir for compressed air and why?

a] rotary compressor to avoid pulsating effect

b] reciprocating compressor to avoid pulsating effect

c] both rotary and reciprocating compressors to avoid pulsating effect

d] none of the above

221) Which of the following factors is/are considered while selecting a compressor?

a] type of oil filter required

b] volumetric efficiency

c] viscosity of the liquids used

d] all of the above

222) Which of the following is a component used in air generation system?

a] pressure switch

b] pressure gauge

c] drier

d] intercooler

223) Where is an intercooler connected in a two stage compressor?

a] intercooler is connected after the two stage compressor

b] intercooler is connected between the two stages of the compressor

c] intercooler is connected before the two stage compressor

d] none of the above

224) Which of the following notations is used to represent a regulator unit?

a] 3]0

b] 0]3

c] 3

d] none of the above

225) Which of the following logic valve is known as shuttle valve?

a] OR gate

b] AND gate

c] NOR gate

d] NAND

226) In pneumatic systems, AND gate is also known as

a] check valve

b] shuttle valve

c] dual pressure valve

d] none of the above

227) What is a pressure sequence valve?

a] it is a combination of adjustable pressure relief valve and directional control valve

b] it is a combination of nonadjustable pressure relief valve and directional control valve

c] it is a combination of adjustable pressure reducing valve and check valve

d] it is a combination of adjustable pressure reducing valve and flow control valve

228) Overlapping of signals in pneumatic systems can be avoided by using

a] rolling lever valve

b] idle roller lever valve

c] both a] and b]

d] none of the above

229) Which of the following statements is true for cascade method which is used to draw a pneumatic circuit?

a] signal processing valves are connected in parallel

b] when the number of signal processing valves are greater than 4, the signals are strong

c] cascade method does not consider the cost factor

d] all of the above

230) What is the part, shown in below diagram of 3/2 valve, called?

a] manually operated valve

b] pilot operated valve

c] pressure electric converter

d] none of the above

231) In which systems, spool of the servo valve is operated by a torque motor?

a] hydromechanical servo systems

b] electrohydraulic servo systems

c] conventional servo valve

d] all of the above

232) What does servo mean in servo valve system?

a] it cannot receive a feedback but the desired output can be obtained

b] it cannot receive a feedback and the desired output cannot be obtained

c] it can receive a feedback and the desired output can be obtained

d] none of the above

233) In conventional valves, which component is used to move the spool?

a] torque motor

b] mechanical servo valve

c] solenoid

d] all of the above

234) What is the advantage of DC solenoid coils?

a] DC solenoid coils have high rush in current

b] DC solenoid coils have constant level of current

c] DC solenoid coils have rating of 220 V DC

d] all of the above

235) Which of the following statements is true for a proportional valve?

a] spool of the proportional valve can travel maximum length

b] digital type of functioning is possible in proportional valve

c] proportional valve requires a separate flow control valve

d] all of the above

236) Which of the following statements is/are false?

a] air is non-compressible

b] less power is developed in fluid power systems than conventional systems

c] mechanical linkages used for load handling purposes have high efficiency

d] all of the above

237) The hydraulic system is

a] less precise than pneumatic system

b] more precise than pneumatic system

c] both hydraulic and pneumatic systems are same on basis of precision

d] none of the above

238) Which energy is used to transmit power in hydrostatic system?

a] pressure energy

b] kinetic energy

c] potential energy

d] all of the above

239) Which system uses kinetic energy to transmit power?

a] hydrostatic system

b] hydrodynamic system

c] pneumatic system

d] none of the above

240) If no load is attached to piston rod, the movement of piston assembly is possible when

a] oil overcomes its self weight

b] oil overcomes friction in the piston rod assembly

c] both a] and b]

d] none of the above

241) Which factor helps in obtaining high speed of the piston rod in the hydraulic system?

a] decreased friction

b] pump capacity

c] increased flow rate

d] all of the above

242) During any operation in hydraulic system, oil prefers the path of

a] least resistance

b] maximum resistance

c] both a] and b]

d] none of the above

243) In a hydraulic circuit a pump is provided with two outlet paths, one where load is attached and other to the reservoir] Which path will the oil choose to flow first?

a] oil will flow to the path where load is attached

b] oil will flow back to the reservoir first

c] oil will flow through both the paths simultaneously

d] none of the above

244) Which of the following is used as an accessory in hydraulic power unit?

a] pumps

b] valves

c] motor

d] reservoir

245) Which type of pump is used for lifting water from the ground surface to the top of the building?

a] centrifugal pump

b] turbine pump

c] submersible pump

d] all of the above

246) Pumps used in hydraulic applications are

a] positive displacement pumps

b] variable displacement pumps

c] fixed displacement pumps

d] all of the above

247) What is a positive displacement pump?

a] oil from suction side of the pump flows completely to the delivery side

b] volume of fluid discharged cannot return back to the suction side of the pump

c] discharges fixed volume of fluid every cycle

d] all of the above

248) While operating a positive displacement pump,

a] the shut-off valve should be closed on delivery side

b] the shut-off valve should be closed on suction side

c] the shut-off valve should be opened on delivery side

d] none of the above

249) What effect does working pressure have on input power for radial piston pumps?

a] as working pressure increases input power decreases

b] as working pressure increases input power increases

c] pressure remains constant for different input powers

d] none of the above

250) Radial piston pumps can have,

a] cylinder block rotating and cam stationary

b] cylinder block stationary and cam rotating

c] both a] and b]

d] none of the above

251) Why are hydraulic cylinders cushioned?

a] cushioning decelerates the piston of a cylinder

b] stress and vibrations can be reduced

c] both a] and b]

d] none of the above

252) Which of the following statements is true?

a] Tie-rod cylinders are used in applications having working pressure of 70 bar

b] Welded type cylinders are used in systems having working pressure more than 70 bar

c] Tie-rod cylinders can be used in systems having working pressure more than 70 bar

d] all of the above

253) Which of these actions does a hydraulic cylinder perform?

a] pushing

b] lifting

c] both a] and b]

d] none of the above

254) Leakage in welded type of hydraulic cylinder is prevented by

a] wiper in gland cover

b] rod seal in end cover

c] rod seal in gland cover

d] none of the above

255)In single acting hydraulic cylinders the piston comes back to its original position due to

a] spring force
b] self-weight
c] momentum of a flywheel
d] all of the above
256) Check valve is a type of
a] pressure reducing valve
b] pressure relief valve
c] directional control valve
d] none of the above
257) A pressure relief valve can be
a] direct operated
b] pilot operated
c] solenoid operated
d] all of the above
258) How is reverse flow possible in pilot operated check valve?
a] spring force lifts the ball due to which reverse flow is possible
b] fluid pressure lifts the ball due to which reverse flow is possible
c] both a] and b]
d] none of the above
259) What is the difference between pressure relief valve and pressure reducing valve?
a] pressure reducing valve is connected between pump and tank line while pressure relief valve is connected between DCV and branch circuit
b] pressure relief valve is always normally opened
c] pressure reducing valve is connected between DCV and branch circuit while pressure relief valve is connected between pump and tank
d] none of the above
260) Accumulator used in gas charged accumulator is
a] hydraulic
b] pneumatic
c] hydropneumatic
d] none of the above
261) What is the function of pressure switch?
a] pressure switch is used to start a motor
b] pressure switch is used to stop a motor
c] pressure switch is used to de-energize a solenoid
d] all of the above
262) Intensifier used in pneumatic systems has output pressure

a] less than input pressure

b] more than input pressure

c] same as input pressure

d] none of the above

263) What is the function of unloading relief valve and can it be used as an accessory for accumulators?

a] unloading relief valve is used to charge the accumulator by a pump when accumulator pressure falls below the set value and it can be used as an accessory]

b] unloading relief valve is used to charge the accumulator by a pump when accumulator pressure falls below the set value but is not used as an accessory

c] unloading relief valve is used to charge the accumulator by a pump when accumulator pressure rises above the set value but is not used as an accessory

d] unloading relief valve is used to charge the accumulator by a pump when accumulator pressure rises above the set value and is used as an accessory

264) Cylinder has a bore area of 300 cm 2 and velocity of 180 cm/min] Calculate the flow rate of a pump

a] 55 l/min

b] 50 l/min

c] 54 l/min

d] none of the above

265) Which of the following statements is true, for two pumps used in circuit when initially fast operation is performed to reach a job and feeding operation is done at a slow speed?

a] initially to reach a job, a tool must be connected to a pump of high discharge and low pressure

b] initially to reach a job, a tool must be connected to a pump of low discharge and high pressure

c] for feeding operation low discharge low pressure pump is required

d] none of the above

266) What are different operations performed by PLC's?

a] Boolean logic

b] Timing

c] Arithmetic

d] all of the above

267) Which of the following pumps saves more power?

a] single pump

b] double pump

c] single and double pump use same amount of power

d] none of the above

268) What is the advantage of PLC?

a] easy to find errors

b] replacements can be easily made

c] PLC's are easily programmed

d] all of the above

269) Mass of water vapour in unit volume of air is known as

a] relative humidity

b] absolute humidity

c] saturation quantity

d] none of the above

270) Which valve is also known as memory valve?

a] single pilot signal valve

b] double pilot signal valve

c] roller lever valve

d] logic valve

271) What is the difference between signal air and control air?

a] signal air actuates final control valve and control air flows to the cylinder through the final control valve for forward and backward movement of piston rod

b] control air actuates final control valve and signal air flows to the cylinder through the final control valve for forward and backward movement of piston rod

c] both a] and b]

d] none of the above

272) Which of the following is used to sense the initial and final positions of a piston rod?

a] lever operated direction control valve

b] limit switch

c] roller lever valve

d] all of the above

273) Which valve gets activated only in one direction that is forward or backward movement of the piston rod?

a] roller lever valve

b] idle roller lever valve

c] both a] and b]

d] none of the above

274) Which numbers are used to denote retraction of a piston rod?

a] even numbers

b] odd numbers

c] both even and odd numbers

d] none of the above

275) Which of the following is an element of time delay valve?

a] flow control valve

b] direction control valve

c] both a] and b] d] none of the above

d] none of above

276) Which of the following is a type of cushioning in hydraulic cylinders?

a] trunnion cushioning

b] adjustable cushioning

c] clevis cushioning

d] none of the above

277) How is proximity switch differentiated from limit switch?

a] proximity switch is activated when moving parts have physical contact with it

b] proximity switch is activated when non-moving parts have physical contact

c] proximity switch is activated when moving parts are close to it

d] none of the above

278) Which of the following statements is true?

a] electromagnetic relays have high reliability at more cost

b] electromagnetic relays use low current and voltage, to have open or close contact in high voltage and current circuit

c] air pressure passed to pressure electric converter opens a contact which energizes a circuit for the flow of electric contact

d] all of the above

279) In which circuits, relay of low voltage and low current is used to make open or close contact?

a] high voltage and high current circuit

b] low voltage and low current circuit

c] high voltage and low current circuit

d] low voltage and low current circuit

280) In electropneumatic circuits,

a] spool is shifted by signal air

b] spool is shifted by control air

c] spool is shifted by electromotive force

d] all of the above

281) Why are electromechanical relays more popular than solid state relays?

a] they are reliable

b] less costly

c] both a] and b]

d] none of the above

282) In which control valve energy consumption reduces as load decreases?

a] conventional direction control valve

b] proportional direction control valve

c] both a] and b]

d] none of the above

283) Which of the following is a characteristic of servo valve?

a] open loop system

b] closed loop system

c] less contamination

d] all of the above

284) What is PLC?

a] Process logic control

b] Programmable language converter

c] Programmable logic control

d] Programmable logic converter

285) What causes burning of AC solenoid coil?

a] holding current

b] in rush current

c] current clamps

d] all of the above

286) When PLC connections are used instead of electrical connections, the order of operations to be performed can be interchanged by

a] changing hardwired connections

b] changing sequence of program

c] both a] and b]

d] none of the above

287) The heat generated in hydraulic systems can be absorbed by

a] lubrication

b] cooling

c] sealing

d] all of the above

288) For which of the following purpose hydraulic film acts as a seal between the machined cavity and spool?

a] to reduce leakage

b] for cooling purposes

c] for lubrication purposes

d] all of the above

289) Pressure applied on a fluid in a container is equally distributed in all directions and acts with

a] equal force on equal areas parallelly

b] equal force on different areas and at right angles

c] equal force on equal areas and at right angles

d] none of the above

290) Which law explains the behavior of hydraulic fluids under pressure?

a] Charles's law

b] Newtons law

c] Pascal's law

d] none of the above

291) Flow of oil in a pipe takes place due to

a] balanced forces

b] unbalanced forces

c] both balanced and unbalanced forces

d] none of the above

292) Pressure drop in pipes, occurs due to

a] frictional resistance

b] load

c] flow pattern

d] none of the above

293) How is laminar flow characterized in a straight pipe?

a] flow of high shear stress

b] flow of high velocity

c] flow of low-velocity

d] none of the above

294) Positive displacement pump used in hydraulic systems have

a] high viscosity of fluids

b] low efficiency

c] required volume of fluid cannot be discharged

d] all of the above

295) Electric motor has a speed of 1200 rpm and output rate of pump is 6 cc/rev] Calculate flow rate of pump in l/min

a] 6 l/min

b] 7]2 l/min

c] 5 l/min

d] none of the above

296) Calculate the power absorbed by the pump if, it has a flow rate of 20 cc/rev and develops a maximum pressure of 70 bar, when electric motor runs at a speed of 1200 rpm]

a] 1]9 kW

b] 2]8 kW

c] 2]3 kW

d] none of the above

297) Volumetric efficiency is the ratio of

a] theoretical flow rate to actual flow rate

b] actual flow rate to theoretical flow rate

c] actual fluid power to pump input power

d] none of the above

298) Which of the following is a hydrodynamic pump?

a] vane pump

b] centrifugal pump

c] gear pump

d] piston pump

299) What causes reduction in speed of the piston rod when the hydraulic cylinder is cushioned?

a] oil flow through small space

b] back pressure created in the system

c] both a] and b

d] none of the above

300) Which of the following is a hydraulic cylinder based on application?

a] welded

b] bolted

c] ram

d] all of the above

301) What happens when supply of oil to a single acting cylinder is stopped?

a] no pressure is exerted on the system

b] more pressure is exerted on the piston

c] less pressure is exerted on the piston

d] none of the above

302) When does expansion of spring and retraction of cylinder take place in spring type single acting cylinder?

a] oil pressure exerted is less than spring compression pressure

b] oil pressure exerted is more than spring compression pressure

c] oil pressure exerted and spring compression pressure are same

d] none of the above

303) In a telescopic cylinder, as the number of stages increase

a] diameter of piston rod also increases

b] diameter of piston rod decreases

c] diameter of the piston rod remains the same

d] none of the above

304) Why are bleed off circuits used?

a] bleed off circuit is used to restrict the flow of fluid into the hydraulic cylinder

b] bleed off circuit is used to restrict the flow of fluid out of the hydraulic cylinder

c] bleed off circuits are used to reduce the speed of actuator

d] all of the above

305) Which of the following is applicable for bleed off circuits?

a] bleed off circuits develop heat in the system

b] bleed off circuits are used for resistive loads

c] bleed off circuits are used for runaway loads

d] all of the above

306) What is the function of sequence valve used in hydraulic circuits?

a] sequence valves are used to perform number of operations one after the other after the set pressure is reached

b] sequence valves are used to perform number of operations continuously before the set pressure is reached

c] sequence valves after reaching set pressure oil is flown to the tank

d] all of the above

307) When is a pressure reducing valve used?
a] it is used when higher pressure than system pressure is required
b] it is used when lower pressure than system pressure is required
c] when absolutely zero pressure is required
d] all of the above

308) How is strong magnetic field in a solenoid achieved?
a] strong magnetic field in a solenoid is achieved, if coil acts as conductor
b] coil is surrounded by a iron frame
c] iron core is placed at the centre of the coil
d] all of the above

309) What is the DC range of of solenoids in pneumatic systems?
a] 12 V and 24 V
b] 110 V and 220 V
c] both a] and b]
d] none of the above

310) Which of the following is used an output device on a ladder diagram?
a] proximity sensor
b] detent switch
c] relay
d] all of the above

311) The output device on a ladder diagram is represented by
a] square
b] circle
c] rectangle
d] semicircle

312) In mnemonics instructions, what does I in LDI indicate?
a] switch is normally open
b] switch is normally closed
c] it indicates operating of second switch
d] none of the above

313) In industrial applications hydraulic fluids have viscosity grade ranging from
a] 20 to 50
b] 70 to 95
c] 46 to 68
d] 15 to 44

314) High viscosity fluids have

a] low pressure drop
b] less power consumption
c] slow operation
d] all of the above

315) What is viscosity index?
a] effect of pressure on changes in viscosity
b] effect of temperature on changes in viscosity
c] effect of resistance between two surfaces
d] none of the above

316) Which property decides the behavior of fluid when mixed with water?
a] pour point
b] demulsibility
c] viscosity
d] oxidation

317) For any operation in a hydraulic system the fluid should have pour point
a] 20 0F below the lowest temperature
b] 20 0F above the lowest temperature
c] 20 0C below the lowest temperature
d] 20 0C above the lowest temperature

318) What is the disadvantage of petroleum based fluids?
a] low flash point
b] low density
c] light weight
d] all of the above

319) How is the water content in High Water Fluids (HFA) compared to oil content?
a] more oil than water
b] oil and water are in same proportion
c] more water than oil
d] contains only water

320) A fluid used in hydraulic systems should have
a] low oxidation resistance
b] high oxidation resistance
c] high oxidation enhancing ability
d] none of the above

321) At which pressure, petroleum oil used in hydraulic systems gets compressed by 1/2%?

a] 70 bar

b] 40 bar

c] 30 bar

d] 95 bar

322) What is the relation between temperature and specific weight for water glycol?

a] as temperature increases specific weight decreases

b] as temperature increases specific weight increases

c] temperature and specific weight vary linearly

d] none of the above

323) What is the relation between temperature and viscosity for hydraulic oil?

a] temperature and viscosity vary linearly

b] as temperature decreases viscosity decreases at atmospheric pressure

c] as temperature increases viscosity decreases at atmospheric pressure

d] none of the above

324) High Water Fluids contain

a] oil in water

b] water in oil

c] only water

d] none of the above

325) Viscosity of High Water Fluid is

a] greater than water

b] less than water

c] nearby water

d] none of the above

326) Adding an additive to water glycol fluids improves

a] flammability

b] viscosity

c] oxidation

d] all of the above

327) What is the characteristic of turbulent flow?

a] high velocity

b] the direction of flow and movement of particles is same

c] change in cross section does not affect the flow

d] all of the above

328) Which flow pattern gets affected when cross section of the pipe is changed?

a] laminar flow

b] turbulent flow

c] laminar and turbulent

d] none of the above

329) Speed of the actuator is affected by

a] cross-section area of the orifice

b] velocity of flow

c] pipe diameter

d] all of the above

330) In which of these applications Bernoulli's principle is widely used?

a] design of blowers

b] design of aircraft wings

c] design of propellers

d] all of the above

331) The total energy developed by the hydraulic oil in a system is given as

a] Total energy = (Potential energy + Pressure energy)

b] Total energy = (Potential energy + Kinetic energy)

c] Total energy = (Potential energy – Kinetic energy)

d] none of the above

332) If a pump gives higher flow rate to the valve then, pressure drop in the valve

a] increases

b] decreases

c] remains the same

d] none of the above

333) In Reynolds number (?vd) / µ, the letter µ denotes

a] kinematic viscosity

b] absolute viscosity

c] coefficient of friction

d] none of the above

334) The ratio of inertia force to viscosity is known as

a] Biot number

b] Reynold number

c] Cauchy number

d] Euler number

335) The Reynolds number for laminar flow is

a] more than 2800

b] more than 2000

c] less than 2000

d] between 2000 and 2800]

336) A pipe has a diameter of 0]2 m in which a fluid flows with a velocity of 0]3 m3/s] Determine whether the flow is laminar or turbulent calculating the Reynolds number] Assume kinematic viscosity = 0]5 × 10-4 m2 /s]

a] the flow is laminar having Reynolds number 1200

b] the flow is turbulent having Reynolds number 2100

c] the flow is laminar having Reynolds number 2200

d] the flow is neither laminar nor turbulent

337) What is the advantage of internal gear pump?

a] moderate speed

b] medium pressure

c] high viscosity fluids can be used

d] all of the above

338) The rotation of which inner element causes the liquid to pump out in centrifugal pumps?

a] internal gear

b] rotation of the impeller

c] cylinder rotor

d] none of the above

339) Which force causes vanes to come out of the rotor slots?

a] centripetal force

b] centrifugal force

c] friction force

d] none of the above

340) Which of the following statements is true?

a] combination of stator with rotor is known as cartridge unit

b] combination of stator with vanes is known as cartridge unit

c] combination of rotor with vanes is known as cartridge unit

d] none of the above

341) What is the advantage of flexible vane pump?

a] they can handle solids which are of large size

b] they can create good vacuum

c] both a] and b]

d] none of the above

342) Cartridge kits generate pumping chambers of various sizes, which

a] increase the flow rate

b] decrease the flow rate

c] increase and decrease the flow rate

d] none of the above

343) Which of the following statements is false for vane pumps?

a] wear in contact surfaces occurs due to continuous contact between vane tips and the cam ring

b] different sizes of cartridge kits can be replaced in same vane pump

c] elliptical cam ring is replaced by round cam ring to reduce unbalanced forces

d] none of the above

344) Balanced vane pumps are designed to have

a] fixed displacement

b] variable displacement

c] both fixed and variable displacement

d] none of the above

345) Cam ring of unbalanced vane pump is

a] round

b] elliptical

c] both a] and b]

d] none of the above

346) Which type of displacement is observed in gear pumps?

a] only variable displacement

b] only fixed displacement

c] both fixed and variable displacement

d] none of the above

347) What is the principle of operation used in gear pumps?

a] two gears rotate in same direction

b] two gears rotate in opposite direction

c] both a] and b]

d] none of the above

348) What causes suction of fluid into the gear pump?

a] when pressure drops during disengagement of teeth at the suction side

b] when pressure increases during disengagement of teeth at the suction side c] when pressure drops during engagement of teeth at the suction side

d] when pressure increases during engagement of teeth at the suction side

349) How is the smooth and continuous discharge of fluid achieved in a gear pump?

a] increasing number of teeth

b] decreasing number of teeth

c] none of the above

d] all of above

350) The rotation of gears in internal gear pump takes place in

a] same direction

b] different direction

c] none of the above

d] all of above

351) How does the fluid flow in internal gear pump?

a] fluid enters the suction side between rotor, which is a large exterior gear and idler which is a small interior gear

b] fluid enters the suction side between rotor, which is a small exterior gear and idler which is a large interior gear

c] fluid enters the suction side between rotor and idler which rotate in different directions

d] none of the above

352) What causes internal leakage in internal gear pump?

a] less tolerance level between the meshing surfaces

b] more tolerance level between the meshing surfaces

c] no tolerance between the meshing surfaces

d] none of the above

353) What is the relation between pressure and overall efficiency for a gear pump?

a] as pressure increases, overall efficiency decreases

b] as pressure increases, overall efficiency increases

c] overall efficiency is not affected by change in pressure

d] cannot say

354) Which of the following statements is true for standard hydraulic cylinder and a telescopic cylinder?

a] telescopic and standard cylinders give same stroke length

b] telescopic cylinders give lesser stroke length than standard cylinder

c] telescopic cylinders give greater stroke length than standard cylinder

d] none of the above

355) Telescopic cylinders have

a] only two stage units

b] only three stage units

c] two or three stage units

d] multistage units

356) Which type of hydraulic cylinder has one piston connected to piston rod extended on both the sides of the cylinder?

a] telescopic cylinder

b] tandem cylinder

c] both a] and b]

d] none of the above

357) Which factor decides the working pressure of a hydraulic cylinder?

a] diameter of circular flange

b] bore diameter of cylinder

c] stroke length

d] all of the above

358) Which factor is considered while selecting the diameter of piston rod in hydraulic cylinder?

a] bore diameter

b] length of stroke

c] load

d] all of the above

359) Which end of the hydraulic cylinder, the male clevis is mounted on?

a] cap end

b] rod end

c] both a] and b]

d] none of the above

360) Which of the following is used for mounting purpose in hydraulic cylinders?

a] Female clevis

b] Circular flange

c] Trunnion

d] all of the above

361) How does cushioning affect the speed of the piston when the cylinder is cushioned at extreme end?

a] cushioning decreases the speed of piston near the extreme ends of the cylinder

b] cushioning increases the speed of piston near the extreme ends of the cylinder

c] cushioning increases the speed of piston at the beginning of the stroke in the cylinder

d] cushioning decreases the speed of piston at the beginning of the stroke in the cylinder

362) In adjustable type of cushioning,

a] piston rod can be moved at very slow speed

b] piston rod can be moved at increased speed

c] both a] and b]

d] none of the above

363) Which formula is used to calculate head loss in valves?

a] K2 (v / 2 g)

b] K (v / 2 g)

c] K (v2 / 2 g)

d] none of the above

364) What is the difference between vane pump and radial piston pump?

a] in radial piston pump, radial slots in vane pumps are replaced by radial bores which accommodate pistons

b] in radial piston pump, radial slots in vane pumps are replaced by radial bores which accommodate swash plate

c] in radial piston pump, radial slots in vane pumps are replaced by radial bores which accommodate both swash plate and pistons

d] none of the above

365) How many strokes does a single piston pump need to discharge oil?

a] one stroke

b] two strokes

c] three strokes

d] none of the above

366) How is the arrangement of pistons in piston pumps?

a] axially

b] radially

c] both a] and b]

d] none of the above

367) In which of these pumps, swash plate is used to translate the motion of rotating shaft into reciprocating motion?

a] radial piston pumps
b] axial piston pump
c] bent axis piston pump
d] all of the above

368) Which factors are considered while designing a axial piston pump?
a] use of swash plate
b] application in open loop or closed loop circuit
c] design of bent axis piston pump
d] all of the above

369) Angle of swash plate in axial piston pump is adjusted by
a] compensator
b] yoke
c] both a] and b]
d] none of the above

370) In axial piston pump, the yoke is pushed away from cylinder block due to which,
a] yoke angle increases
b] swash plate angle decreases
c] both a] and b]
d] none of the above

371) When the angle of swash plate decreases
a] flow rate increases
b] flow rate decreases
c] flow rate does not depend on swash plate angle
d] none of the above

372) What will be the discharge of oil in axial piston pump, when the angle of swash plate is zero?
a] discharge of oil is maximum
b] discharge of oil is minimum
c] there is no discharge of oil
d] none of the above

373) A bent axis piston pump has
a] pump axis bent
b] cylinder block which is inclined at an angle to the drive shaft
c] both a] and b]
d] none of the above

374) In which of these pumps, swash plate is replaced by cylinder block?
a] bent axis piston pump

b] radial piston pump

c] axial piston pump

d] none of the above

375) What happens when the distance between flange and cylinder block is varied?

a] piston displacement cannot be varied

b] variable flow rate of fluid can be achieved

c] fixed flow rate can be achieved

d] all of the above

376) What is the maximum angle between cylinder block and shaft axis?

a] 30o

b] 50o

c] 45o

d] all of the above

377) When does holding piston keep the angle between yoke and cylinder block maximum?

a] when set pressure is greater than load pressure

b] when set pressure is less than load pressure

c] when set pressure and load pressure are same

d] all of the above

378) Low-torque high-speed motors are used in

a] cranes

b] winches

c] fans

d] all of the above

379) Which motor causes heavy loads due to its usage in order to move at constant lower speeds?

a] Low-torque high-speed motors

b] High-torque low-speed motors

c] both a] and b]

d] none of the above

380) Motors used in high speed applications have

a] high torque with high speed

b] low torque with high speed

c] high torque with low speed

d] none of the above

INDUSTRIAL TRAINING INSTITUTE

Monthly Test-1, Marks- 20, Date:- ______________

(Every Question Carry Two Marks)

06] A slot is cut halfway across the nut.

A] Locking plate

B] Wire lock

C] Self-locking nut

D] Sawn nut

07] Prevents slackening of two bolts.

A] Locking plate

B] Wire lock

C] Self-locking nut

D] Sawn nut

08] Prevents rotation of the top nut.

A] Lock-nut

B] Grooved nut

C] Self-locking nut

D] Sawn nut

09] Prevents loosening of nut by the use of a plate shaped to fit the nut.

A] Locking plate

B] Wire lock

C] Self-locking nut

D] Sawn nut

10] Hexagonal nut with the lower part made cylindrical and the recessed groove.

A] Lock-nut

B] Grooved nut

C] Self-locking nut

D] Sawn nut

11] Threading tools are checked for accuracy for the 60◦ angle by using a

A] Thread plug gauge

B] centre gauge

C] screw pitch gauge

D] tool angle gauge

12] The number of threads per inch can be checked with a

A] tool gauge

B] metric rule by counting

C] ring gauge

D] screw pitch gauge

13] What is the angle of pipe thread?

A] 60°
B] 47‘/2°
C] 29°
D] 55°.
14] What is the use of pipe thread?
A] transmission
B] maintain pressure
C] airtight connections
D] none of the above.
15] What is the depth of the 2" pipe thread?
A] 0.5"
B] 0.640“
C] 0.335"
D] 0.580".

INDUSTRIAL TRAINING INSTITUTE

Monthly Test-2, Marks- 20, Date:- ______________

(Every Question Carry Two Marks)

16] External Thread provide on Rod or Pipe , by Die and Cutting Tool is called ......
(A] Tapping
(B] Dieing
(C] Threading
(D] Grooving
17] The angle 0f lS thread (V shaped] is ----------
A] 29°
B] 47 1/4°
C] 50°
D] 60
18] ln which of the following methods, only external threads are made -------
A] Form tool mEthOd
B] Compound rest method
C] Tailstock offset method
D] Taper turning attachment method.
19] The surface joining the crest and the root of a thread is known as ----
A] Flank
B] Shank
C] Pitch surface

D] All Of these

20] Pitch of a two start thread is 4 mm. Then the lead of the thread is given by -----

A] 4mm

B] 2mm

C] 8mm

D] 6mm

21] The Gear ratio required for cutting a screw thread of 2.5 mm on a lathe having a lead screw pitch using single point cutting tool is ----

A] 1:2

B] 2:1

C] 1:1 mm

22] The depth of cut for M24 x 3 mm internal thread is

A] 0.5412 x 3

B] 0.6134 x 3

C] 0.5 x 3

D] 0.7 x 3

23] To cut 24 x 3 mm internal acme threads, the core diameter of the job is

A] 20.00 mm

B] 21.66 mm

C] 21.00 mm

D] 20.60 mm

24] The depth of cut for metric square threading is

A] 0.6 x P

B] 0.5 x P

C] 0.5412 x P

D] 0.6412 x P

25] To cut buttress thread, the depth of cut is

A] 0.5412 x P

B] 0.6 x P

C] 0.7 x P

D] 0.75 x P

INDUSTRIAL TRAINING INSTITUTE

Monthly Test-3, Marks- 20, Date:- _______________

(Every Question Carry Two Marks)

26] What is template?

A] One of the cutting operation

B] One of the form turning
C] same figure of the job
D] one of the tool
27] Which purpose use template?
A] For marking & checking
B] for threading
C] for turning
D] for measuring
28] Which material is use for making template?
A] H.C.S. plate
B] Special tool steel
C] brass or copper
d] G.I. sheet or M.S. thin sheet
29] ---------------is used for checking shape of component
A] Template
B] Snap gauge
C] Instrument
D] Sine bar
30] For face copying......... Type template is used
A] Rounded
B] Plate type
C] Flat
D] Triangular
31] The accuracy of a taper is generally checked by means of......
A] taper gauges
B] gauge blocks
C] indicator and height gauge
32] External tapers are checked with
A] limit plug gauge
B] taper ring gauge
C]taper plug gauge
D] thread plug gauge.

33] To check the dimensional accuracy of identical components, a dial test indicator is set-for t 6 Size and used as a comparator. What will you use to set to the dial test indicator?

A] Dial test indicator
B] Teeter gauge
C] Slip gauge

D], surface gauge

34] Sine bar is used for

A] levelling the job for drilling

B] finding the angle of taper job

C] measuring diameter of holes

D] checking profile of thread.

35] Length of sine bar is the distance between

A] one end to another end of sine bar

B] diagonal cross length of the sine bar

C] centre to centre between rollers

D] outside to outside between rollers.

INDUSTRIAL TRAINING INSTITUTE

Monthly Test-4, Marks- 20, Date:- ______________

(Every Question Carry Two Marks)

36] The size of a sine bar is specified by it's

A] weight

B] measurement of width

C] length

D] maximum angle of setting.

37]The purpose of providing a stopper at one end of the sine bar is for

A] easy handling

B] preventing the job from slipping .

C] supporting the slip gauge

D] using as a reference while setting.

38] A sine bar is made with four or five equally'spaced holes on its body. The purpose of these holes is to

A] Handle the sine bar easily

B] Reduce the weight of sin bar

C] Prevent distortion of the top surface of sine bar

D] Give good appearance to the sine bar

39] A sine bar is used for

A] Measuring the diameter of holes '

B] Finding the angle of a taper job

C] Leveling the job for drilling

D] Chuckin'g the profile of a thread

40] For measuring angles using the sine bar the angle framed according to the ratio between the height of slip gauge and the

A] Height of sine bar

B] Number slip gauge
C] Length of sine bar
D] Width of sine bar
41] -----------is used for checking angle within an accuracy of 1.
A] Gauge
B] Sine bar
C] Temple
D] Telescopic gauge
42] Centre line of the contact rollers and datum surface if the sine bar are
A] Same line' '
B] Parallel
C] Inclined
D] Perpendicular
43] The sine bar is made of -.
A] High carbon steel
B] Stabilized chromium steel '
C] High speed steel
D] Nicked steel
44] A sine bar with a length of l=200mm is used to check accurately the angle of a Work piece. The angle to be checked: 250 calculate the height 'h' of the slip gauges?
A] 84.54mm
B] 83.52mm
C] 81.81mm
D] 85.52mm
45] Which of the following statement is correct?'
A] Gauges are used to check the size
B] Template are used to chuck-the size
C] Gauges are used to measure the size
D] Gauges are used to check shape of component

INDUSTRIAL TRAINING INSTITUTE

Monthly Test-5, Marks- 20, Date:- _______________

(Every Question Carry Two Marks)

46] At what standard temperature are the gauges kept in the section?
A] 100 C
B] 20° C
C] 100 F

D] 20° F

47] Which grade of slip gauge is generally used in workshop?

A] Grade 0

B] Grade l

C] Grade H

D] Grade 0

48] As per Indian Standards a special set gauge is used consisting of

A] 81 Pieces

B] 112 Pieces

C] 120 Pieces

D] 130 Pieces

49] The accuracy of reference gauge is

A] 0.05 mm

B] 0.01 mm

C] 0.001 .

D] 0.0001 mm

50] ln case of ant burr on slip gauge, it should be removed by

A] Filling

B] Lapping

C] Scraping

D] Grinding

51] Hardness of slip gauge should be?

A] More than 63 HRC

B] 58 HRC

C] 55 HRC

D] 50 HRC

52]------------- Slip gauge is used for Checking component within an accuracy of 0.01 mm.

A] Workshop gauge

B] Inspection gauge

C] Reference gauge

D] Ring gauge

53], ------------is used for checking accuracy of precision instrument.

A] Gauge block

B] Fader gauge

C] Sine bar

D] Plug gauge

54] Slip gauge are Cleaned before using to ensure accuracy. What medium will you use for this purpose.

A] Oil

B] Thinner

C] Carbon tetrachloride/ White petrol

D] Turpentine oil

55]To check the dimensional accuracy of identical components, a dial test indicator is set-for t 6 Size and used as a comparator. What will you use to set to the dial test indicator?

A] Dial test indicator

B] Teeter gauge

C] Slip gauge

D], surface gauge

INDUSTRIAL TRAINING INSTITUTE

Monthly Test-6, Marks- 20, Date:- _______________

(Every Question Carry Two Marks)

56] which one of the following statement about Sine bar is not correct?

A] Uses tow precision rollers kept on either side

B] Made of the Chromium steel

C] The surface is lapped

D] The centrelines of the holes will be inclined to the top surface

57] A slip gauge is a ---------

A] Rectangular block

B] Square block

C] Cubic block

D] Cylindrical block

58] In 4th SERIES of slip gauge, which one of the following range is correct in set 46 pieces

A] 1.0 to 9.0 mm.

B] 1.001 101.009 mm

C] 1.01 to 1.09 mm

D]'1.1'to_-1.9mm

59] In 5th SERIES of slip gauge, which one Of the following range is correct in set 46 pieces –

A] 100to 100 mm '

B] 1.001 to 1.009 mm

C] 1.01 to 0.09mrn

D] 11 to 9mm

60] In 2NDS SERIES of slip gauge, which one of the following range IS correct in set of 45 pieces-

A] 1.0 to 9.0 mm

B] 1.001 to 1. 009 mm

C] 1.01 to 1.09 mm

D] 1.1 to 1.9mm

61] In 3RD SERIES of slip gauge, which one of the following range is correct in set 46 pieces –

A] 10.0 to 100 mm

B] 1.001 to 1.009 mm

C] 1.01 to 1.09 mm

D] 1.1 to 1.9 mm

62] In 1ST SERIES of slip gauge, which one of the following range is correct in set 46 pieces –

A] 0.001mm

B] 001mm

C] 0.1mm

D] 1.0mm

63] In 2ned SERIES of slip gauge, which one of the following STEP is correct in set of 46 pieces –

A] 0.001mm

B] 0.01 mm

C] 0.1 mm

D] 1-0 mm

64] In 3rd SERIES of slip gauge, which one of the following STEP Is correct in set 46 pieces

A] 0.001mm

B] 0.01mm

C] 0.1 mm

D] 1.0mm

65] In following which type of tip for cemented carbide treading tool?

A] For clamping on reject tool

B] with brazing on tool

C] With welding on tool

INDUSTRIAL TRAINING INSTITUTE

Monthly Test-7, Marks- 20, Date:- ______________

(Every Question Carry Two Marks)

66] The number of threads per inch can be checked with a

A] tool gauge
B] metric rule by counting
C] ring gauge
D] screw pitch gauge

67] Telescopic gauges are used to measure holes and slots.
A] from 10 mm to 100 mm
B] from 12 mm to 152 mm
C] from 12.7 mm to 152.4 mm
D] none of the above.

68] Small hole gauges are used to measure holes and slots.
A] below 10 mm
B] below 12.7 mm
C] below 20 mm
D] below 20.7 mm.

69] A set of number drill series consists of drills in the following ranges. Indicate the correct range
A] 1 to 40
B] 1 to 50
C] 1 to 80
D] 1 to 100

70] In the number drill series, the smallest drill size is...
A] 0.1 mm
B] 0.35 mm
C] 0.5 mm
D] 0.52 mm

71] In the number drill series, the largest drill size is...
A] 102 mm
B] 5.791 mm
C] 5.613 mm
D] 5.410 mm

72] In the letter drill series, the size of the drill 'A' is equal to ...
A] 13 mm
B] 6.08 mm
C] 6.045 mm
D] 5.944 mm

73] In the letter drill series, the largest drill size is equal to...
A] 10.33 mm
B] 10.490 mm

C] 12.01 mm

D] 15.00 mm

74] The feeler gauge is used for...

A] Checking surface roughness

B] Checking the redius of workpieces

C] Checking the gap between mating parts

D] Checking the accuracy of the hole locators

75] The purpose of relief grooves is to...

A] Maintain the required type of fit

B] Ensure contact between surfaces without any obstruction

C] Make for lubrication

D] Adjust the components for play

INDUSTRIAL TRAINING INSTITUTE

Monthly Test-8, Marks- 20, Date:- ______________

(Every Question Carry Two Marks)

76] Generally gauges are made out of

A] nickel chromium

B] mild steel

C] cast steel

D] H.S.S.

77] Generally gauges are used for

A] mass production

B] measuring the components

C] individual component

D] checking the dimensional accuracy

78] A centre gauge is used to

A] check the pitch of the thread

B] set the tool at the correct centre height

C] check the fit of the thread

D] check the angle of the threading tool

79] A metric centre gauge has an angle of

A] 55◦

B] 60◦

C] 47.5◦

D] 29◦

80] In case of ant burr on slip gauge, it should be removed by

A] Filling

B] Lapping

C] Scraping

D] Grinding

81] The purpose for which lapping operation are carried out ---

A] To refine surface finish.

B] To improve quality of fit

C] To improve geometrical accuracy,

D] All the above

82] Lapping compound material is ----------

A] Sand stone

B] Diamond

C] Quartz

D] Corundum

83] When does the work piece get charged with the abrasive and cut the lap?

A] The work piece is harder than the lap

B] The work piece is softer than the lap

C] The lap is softer than the work piece

D] The lap is coarser than the work piece

84] The grooves are provided on the lapping plate for-----------..

A] Preventing distortion of the plate

B] Retaining lapping paste

C] Reducing friction

D] Collects the metal-chips

85] The following material is used for diamond lapping ....

A] H55

B] Copper ‘

C] Aluminium oxide,

D] High carbon steel

INDUSTRIAL TRAINING INSTITUTE

Monthly Test-9, Marks- 20, Date:- _______________

(Every Question Carry Two Marks)

86] Which one of the following is a cold working process by which improvement of surface finish, dimensional accuracy and work hardening can be affected without removal of metal?

A] Burnishing

B] Honing

C] Lapping _

D] Super finishing

87] In the honing Process, the movement of the spindle is ---‘ ------------

A] Vertical and reciprocating

B] Reciprocating

C] Vertical

D] Horizontal and reciprocating

88] lt is the process carried out by using abrasive stick?

A] Lapping

B] Honing

C] Super finishing

89] This process is carried out in both hardened and unhardened state ------

A] Burnishing

B] Super finishing

C] Lapping

D] Honing

90] Honing process is preferred for -------------.

A] Finishing internal holes

B] Boring of carbides

C] Internal threads cutting ‘

D] External grinding

91] The range of surface roughness in Honing is in the range of --------

A] 0.9 to 5 microns

B] 0.1 to 5 microns

C] 0.13 to 1.25 microns

D] 0 to 100 microns

92] The productivity of honing Operation is

A] Less than the productivity of lapping Operation

B] More than the productivity of lapping operation

C] Equal to the productivity of lapping operation for the same work piece

D] None of these

93] Material For bearing lining.

A] Duralumin

B] Brass

C] Bronze

D] Babbit

94] Unbalanced load.

A] Bearing pinched in the housing.

B] Discolouration of bearing.

C] Spinning of the outer ring in the housing

D] Ball or Roller denting.

95] Housing warped.

A] Bearing pinched in the housing.

B] Discolouration of bearing.

C] Spinning of the outer ring in the housing

D] Ball or Roller denting.

INDUSTRIAL TRAINING INSTITUTE

Monthly Test-10, Marks- 20, Date:- ______________

(Every Question Carry Two Marks)

96] Distorted shaft and other parts of the bearing assembly

A] Bearing pinched in the housing.

B] Discolouration of bearing.

C] Spinning of the outer ring in the housing

D] Ball or Roller denting.

97]Housing bore too large.

A] Bearing pinched in the housing.

B] Discolouration of bearing.

C] Spinning of the outer ring in the housing

D] Ball or Roller denting.

98] Incorrect method of mounting.

A] Bearing pinched in the housing.

B] Discolouration of bearing.

C] Spinning of the outer ring in the housing

D] Ball or Roller denting.

99] Housing bore out of round.

A] Bearing pinched in the housing.

B] Discolouration of bearing.

C] Spinning of the outer ring in the housing

D] Ball or Roller denting.

100] Prevents dust or grit entering into shaft bearings.

A] '0' ring seal

B] Radial lip seal

C] Wiper seal

D] Spring loaded seal

101] Heating plain carbon steel uniformly above the lower critical temperature, casuses the commencement Of the formation of solid solution called...

A] Ferrite

B] Pearlite

C] Austenite

D] Martensite

102] The process of heating and cooling for changing the structure of steel for obtaining the required properties is called...

A] Hardening

B] Heat treatment

C] Normalising

D] Tempering

103] The main purposes of annealing is

A] To increase the hardness

B] To increase the toughness

C] To improve machinability

D] To remove distoration

104] The process which helps in producing a fine grain for uniformity of structure and for improved mechanical properties is known as...

A] Tempering

B] Annealing

C] Hardening

D] Normalising

105] Which one of the following is an alloy of carbon and iron, in which carbon is in a combined state?

A] Steel

B] Wrought iron

C] Cast iron

D] Pig-iron

INDUSTRIAL TRAINING INSTITUTE

Monthly Test-11, Marks- 20, Date:- ______________

(Every Question Carry Two Marks)

183] Most hydraulic circuits:

a) Operate from a central hydraulic power unit

b) Use air-over-oil power units

c) Have a dedicated power unit

d) Does not have dedicated power unit

184] Hydraulic and pneumatic circuits:

a) Perform the same way for all functions

b) Perform differently for all functions

c) Perform the same with some exceptions

d) Does not perform all the functions

185] The lubricator in a pneumatic circuit is the:

a) First element in line

b) Second element in line

c) Last element in line

d) Third element in line

186] When comparing first cost of hydraulic systems to pneumatic systems, generally they are:

a) More expensive to purchase

b) Less expensive to purchase

c) Cost is same

d) Cost is not required

187] When comparing operating cost of hydraulic systems to pneumatic systems, generally they

are.

a) More expensive to operate

b) Less expensive to operate

c) Cost is same to operate

d) Cost is not required

188] The most common hydraulic fluid is:

a) Mineral oil

b) Synthetic fluid

c) Water

d) Gel

189) Which fluid is used in hydraulic power systems?

a] water

b] oil

c] non-compressible fluid

d] all of the above

190) Pressure of 1 bar is equal to

a] 14]5 psi

b] 145 psi

c] 12]5 psi

d] 145 x 10-6 psi

191) What effect does overloading have on fluid power and electrical systems?

a] electrical components get damaged in electrical systems

b] fluid power system stops working without damaging the components

c] both a] and b]

d] none of the above

192) How is power transmitted in fluid power systems?

a] power is transmitted instantaneously

b] power is transmitted gradually

c] both a] and b]

d] none of the above

INDUSTRIAL TRAINING INSTITUTE

Monthly Test-12, Marks- 20, Date:- ______________

(Every Question Carry Two Marks)

193) Generally liquids are non-compressible but when a large pressure of 70 bar is applied, petroleum oil can be compressed up to

a] 0]5% of its original volume

b] 1% of its original volume

c] 5% of its original volume

d] none of the above

194) The resistance offered to the flow of fluid inside a piston develops into

a] pressure

b] force

c] stress

d] all of the above

195) At low pressures, liquids are

a] compressible

b] non-compressible

c] unpredictable

196) In hydraulic systems,

a] the mechanical energy is transferred to the oil and then converted into mechanical energy

b] the electrical energy is transferred to the oil and then converted into mechanical energy

c] the mechanical energy is transferred to the oil and converted into electrical energy

d] none of the above

197) Which of the following is used as a component in hydraulic power unit?

a] pressure gauge
b] filler gauge
c] valve
d] reservoir
198) Rotary motion in a hydraulic power unit is achieved by using
a] hydraulic cylinder
b] pneumatic cylinder
c] both hydraulic and pneumatic cylinder
d] none of the above
199) What is the relation between speed and flow rate for fixed displacement vane pump?
a] flow rate increases with increase in speed of rotor
b] flow rate decreases with increase in speed of rotor
c] flow rate is constant and does not change with change in speed
d] none of the above
200) In fixed displacement vane pump,
a] flow rate decreases with increase in working pressure
b] flow rate increases with increase in working pressure
c] flow rate is constant and does not change with working pressure
d] none of the above
201) Which type of motion is transmitted by hydraulic actuators?
a] linear motion
b] rotary motion
c] both a] and b]
d] none of the above
202) What is the function of electric actuator?
a] converts electrical energy into mechanical torque
b] converts mechanical torque into electrical energy
c] converts mechanical energy into mechanical torque
d] none of the above

9 798887 044590

Printed by Libri Plureos GmbH in Hamburg,
Germany